Teacher's guide
ACTIVE MATHEMATICS 3

B. V. Hony and *D. A. Turner*
Oundle School

CONTENTS

Preface 3

Introduction to Book 3 4

Book 3 and the National Curriculum 6

Answers

| Chapter 1 | ARITHMETIC I 9 |
| | Coursework: Kit Kat bars *13* |

Chapter 2   GRAPHS I *14*
             Coursework: World sprint record *19*

Chapter 3   ALGEBRA I *20*
             Coursework: Motoring costs *24*
             FACT FINDERS: The UK hurricane *25*

Chapter 4   GEOMETRY I *26*
             Coursework: The Cross-staff *29*
             Multiple Choice Tests 1A and 1B *30*

Chapter 5   TRIGONOMETRY *31*
             Coursework: Aviation flight paths *34*

Chapter 6   PROPORTION *35*
             Coursework: The solar system *39*

Chapter 7   ALGEBRA II *40*
             Coursework: The Active Maths puzzle *47*
             FACT FINDERS: The Channel Tunnel *48*
             Multiple Choice Tests 2A and 2B *48*

Chapter 8   GRAPHS II *49*
             Coursework: Bicycle gears *55*

Chapter 9   ARITHMETIC II *56*
             Coursework: World population *60*

Chapter 10   STATISTICS AND PROBABILITY *61*
             Coursework: Traffic flow problem *69*

Chapter 11   GEOMETRY II *71*
             Coursework: Surveying with a Silva compass *79*
             FACT FINDERS: Wimbledon *80*
             Multiple Choice Tests 3A and 3B *80*

Preface

Teachers should find that this book not only contains a set of correct answers to the pupils' text questions but is also a useful resource when teaching from the text. Much of the material is related to everyday situations and this should help teachers to develop the pupils' capacity to use mathematics, as well as to develop their knowledge and understanding of mathematics. Where appropriate, pupils should be encouraged to find out facts for themselves, and the teacher should encourage and promote relevant class discussion on topics being covered in the text.

Teaching mathematics has been likened to the constant ebb and flow of an incoming tide: progress occurs on a broad front with continual covering and recovering of skills until they are understood. This explains why topics in the text have been taken from three levels of the National Curriculum (see the last page of the Contents in the pupils' text). To apply this technique it is important that the material in the text is taught sequentially. The depth to which a topic is covered must be left to the teacher: a weak class might only cover the first half of each Exercise, while a more able class might do the main section in each Exercise and then spend more time on the Masterminders, which are often quite challenging.

Finally it is hoped that teachers will not only find these books easy to use, but that they will enjoy sharing the stimulating and challenging material in them with their pupils. We can only do justice to those who we teach if we are effective in the classroom.

B. V. Hony

D. A. Turner

Oundle 1992

Introduction to Book 3

Presentation and layout of work

The following guide lines, which are used throughout each of the first three texts in this series, enable pupils, particularly the less able, to develop good habits of presentation.

For all work with equations:
[F]   Facts
[E]   Equation
[S]   Substitution
[W]   Working

For all work where words of explanation and working are necessary:
[W]   Words
[W]   Working
[A]   Answer

Features in the textbook

Masterminders and Extensions
These questions are useful to challenge pupils and some will tax the most able. They are extremely useful to occupy those who have finished a piece of work while others are completing theirs.

Revision Exercises
There is a comprehensive Revision Exercise at the end of each chapter, and the content of each covers the topics of the chapter. They can be used either for test or for revision purposes.

Basics Tests
These are at the end of Chapters 1, 4, 5, 8 and 9 and the aim is to give practice at a number of basic skills using three types of computation.

A   Calculator

Pupils should aim to do the six questions without writing anything down except the question number and the answer. (Before the next part of the test calculators must be put away.)

B   Paper and pencil

All working should be shown and a reasonable amount of time given.

C   Mental

First tell the pupils to write down in the margin the numbers 16 to 25 and then tell them that they are to write down only the answer and that all working must be done in their head. Each question must be read out twice.

Aural Tests
These are at the end of Chapters 3, 7 and 10, and aim to give practice in this important examination skill.

Introduction to Book 3

Basic Algebra Tests

These are at the end of Chapters 2, 6 and 11. The first and second of these can be used to assess the ability of the class *before* the Algebra chapters are done.

Multiple Choice Tests

There are six of these tests and between them they cover all the topics in the text. The tests marked 'A' are easier than those marked 'B'. In general, pupils do less well at this type of test and it is often important to insist on full working where necessary.

The tests themselves have been put at the back of the pupils' text so that the pupils are less likely to do the tests beforehand! In this guide the answers to each pair of tests are put at the end of the appropriate block of chapters.

Coursework

At the end of each chapter there is a structured piece of Coursework whose content is directly related to the material of the text.

Courseworks should be done as part of the course and can be done as a whole or in part. They can also be used by the teacher as prepared lessons, or given to the more able pupil who has finished his or her work ahead of the rest of the class.

The technique of writing up Coursework must be taught and it is often a good idea for the teacher to work through one Coursework with a class. The teacher should discuss the advice given to pupils in 'To the user of this book' at the front of the pupils' text.

While a class is doing Coursework, the teacher should be discussing relevant points with pupils, and encouraging them to develop their own ideas and to write down things they notice. The teacher should also check that pupils write up their report as the work progresses and do not leave it to the last few lessons.

Marking Coursework need not be a time-consuming onerous task if impression marking is used. Details of the mark scheme are given in 'To the user of this book' in the pupils' text and the allocation of marks is shown at the top of the worked solutions in this guide.

The National Curriculum

Topics in this text are taken from Levels 6, 7 and 8 of the National Curriculum, and full details are given in the table on the next three pages.

Attainment Target 1 is covered in the Courseworks.

BOOK 3 AND THE NATIONAL CURRICULUM

Attainment Target 2 (Number)

LEVEL 6	Chapter	LEVEL 7	Chapter	LEVEL 8	Chapter
reading, writing and ordering decimals and appreciating place values.	1	multiplying and dividing mentally single-digit multiples of any power of 10, realizing that with a number less than 1 multiplication has a decreasing effect and division an increasing effect.	1	using index notations to represent powers and roots.	1
working out fractional and percentage changes.	1, 9	solving problems using multiplication and division with numbers of any size.	1, 6	expressing and using numbers in standard index form, with positive and negative integer powers of 10.	1
calculating using ratios in a variety of situations.	5, 6	expressing positive integers as a product of primes.	*	substituting negative numbers into formulae involving addition, subtraction, multiplication and division.	3, 7
understanding and using equivalence of fractions and ratios and relating these to decimals and percentages.	1, 6, 9	using the memory and bracket facilities of a calculator to plan a calculation and evaluate expressions.	1	calculating with fractions.	1, 6
converting fractions to decimals and percentages and finding one number as a percentage of another.	1, 9	recognizing that measurement expressed to a given unit is in possible error of half a unit.	9	estimating and approximating to check that the results of caculations are of the right order.	1
using estimation and approximation to check that answers to multiplication and division problems involving whole numbers are of the right order.	1				
recognizing that measurement is approximate and choosing the degree of accuracy appropriate for a particular purpose.	9				
understanding and using compound measures, e.g. speed, density.	1, 2, 6				

Attainment Target 3 (Algebra)

LEVEL 6	Chapter	LEVEL 7	Chapter	LEVEL 8	Chapter
using spreadsheets or other computer facilities to explore number patterns.	*	using symbolic notation to express the rules of sequences.	3	manipulating simple algebraic expressions.	3, 7
determining possible rules for generating sequences.	3	exploring complex number patterns generated by a computer.	*	understanding and using a range of formulae and functions.	3, 7
solving linear equations; solving simple polynomial equations by 'trial and improvement' methods.	7	using the rules of indices for positive integer values.	3, 7, 8	understanding the relationships between powers and roots.	1
using and plotting Cartesian co-ordinates to represent simple mappings.	8, 11	understanding the meaning of reciprocals and exploring relationships.	1, 8	solving a variety of linear and other inequalities.	3, 7

BOOK 3 AND THE NATIONAL CURRICULUM

	Chapter
• generalizing, mainly in words, patterns which arise in various situations, e.g. symmetry of results.	3
• solving simple inequalities on a number line.	3, 7
• solving a range of polynomial equations by 'trial and improvement' methods.	7
• using algebraic methods to solve simultaneous linear equations in two variables.	3
• drawing and interpreting the graphs of linear functions and using graphical methods to solve simultaneous linear equations.	2, 8
• generating various types of graphs on a computer or calculator and interpreting them.	8

LEVEL 7	
• using straight line graphs to locate regions given by linear inequalities.	*
• knowing the form of graphs of simple functions, eg. quadratic, cubic, reciprocal.	8
• understanding the role of a counter example in the context of rules for sequences and in disproving hypotheses.	*

Attainment Target 4 (Shape and space)

LEVEL 6	Chapter
• recognizing and using common 2-D representation of 3-D objects.	11
• reflecting simple shapes in a mirror line.	11
• enlarging a shape by a whole number scale factor.	11
• classifying and defining types of quadrilaterals.	*
• knowing and using angle and symmetry properties of quadrilaterals and other polygons.	4
• using computers to generate and transform 2-D shapes.	11
• devising instructions for a computer to produce desired shapes and paths.	11
• understanding and using bearings to define directions.	11

LEVEL 7	Chapter
• using coordinates to locate position in 3-D.	*
• determining the locus of an object moving subject to a rule.	11
• understanding and applying Pythagoras' theorem.	7
• using knowledge and skills in length, area and volume to carry out calculations in plane and solid shapes.	7
• enlarging a shape by a fractional scale factor.	11

LEVEL 8	Chapter
• understanding and using mathematical similarity; knowing that angles remain unchanged and corresponding sides are in the same ratio.	4, 5
• using sine, cosine and tangent in right-angled triangles, in 2-D.	5
• distinguishing between formulae for perimeter, area and volume by considering dimensions.	*
• understanding and using vector notation.	*

BOOK 3 AND THE NATIONAL CURRICULUM

Attainment Target 5 (Handling data)

LEVEL 6	Chapter	LEVEL 7	Chapter	LEVEL 8	Chapter
• specifying an issue for which data are needed; designing and using observation sheets to collect data; collating and analysing results.	10	• specifying a simple hypothesis; designing and using an appropriate questionnaire to test it; collecting and analysing results to see whether a hypothesis is valid.	*	• designing and using a questionnaire with multiple responses, collating and analysing results to test a hypothesis.	*
• designing and using a questionnaire to survey opinion (taking account of bias), collating and analysing results.	10	• using and recording grouped data with class intervals suitably defined; producing a frequency table; calculating a mean using a calculator.	*	• constructing a cumulative frequency table.	*
• creating scatter graphs for discrete and continuous variables and having a basic understanding of correlation.	10	• finding the mean, median, mode and range of a frequency distribution for given sets of data and interpreting the results.	10	• constructing a cumulative frequency curve using the upper boundary of the class interval, finding the median, upper quartile, lower quartile and inter-quartile range, and interpreting the results.	*
• constructing and interpreting information through two-way tables and network diagrams.	11	• drawing a frequency polygon as a line graph from a frequency distribution for grouped data; making comparisons between two frequency distributions.	10	• understanding that when dealing with two independent events, the probability of them both happening is less than the probability of either of them happening (unless the probability is 0 or 1).	10
• identifying all the outcomes when dealing with two combined events which are independent using diagrammatic, tabular or other forms.	10	• constructing and interpreting flow diagrams with and without loops.	*	• calculating the probability of a combined event given the probability of two independent events and illustrating combined probabilities of several events using tabulation or tree-diagrams.	10
• knowing that the total sum of the probabilities of mutually exclusive events is 1 and that the probability of something happening is 1 minus the probability of it not happening.	10	• drawing a line of 'best fit' by inspection on a scatter diagram.	10		
		• understanding and using relative frequency as an estimate of probability.	10		
		• appreciating, when assigning probabilities, that relative frequency and equally likely considerations may not be appropriate and 'subjective' estimates of probability have to be made.	10		
		• understanding and applying the addition of probabilities for mutually exclusive events.	10		

Chapter 1 ARITHMETIC I

Exercise 1 — page 4

1. a 4.3 b 6.7 c 8.6 d 0.2 e 0.9
   f 1.0 g 0.0 h 0.1 i 0.0
2. a 4.7 b 6.3 c 7.0 d 480 e 310
   f 46 000 g 0.25 h 0.084 i 0.085
3. a 3.62 b 6.08 c 7.70 d 457 e 456
   f 45 700 g 0.123 h 0.136 i 0.0247
4. These can be done mentally
   a 7.2 $7\tfrac{1}{5}$ b 500 c 0.15 $\tfrac{3}{20}$ d 1.8 $1\tfrac{4}{5}$ e 0.08 $\tfrac{2}{25}$
   f 9 g 0.1 $\tfrac{1}{10}$ h 1 i 60 j 200
   k 6000 l 9900
5. a 1000 b 4 c 2 d 4000
   e 0.1 f 10 g 0.04 h 0.3
6. (i) a 1000 b 3.9 c 1.9 d 4200
   e 0.094 f 10 g 0.042 h 0.31
   (ii) a 998 b 3.91 c 1.92 d 4190
   e 0.0937 f 10.4 g 0.0419 h 0.308
7. a 2.4×10^2 b 1.3×10^3 c 5.5×10^3 d 8.5×10^5
   e 2.5×10^{-2} f 1.1×10^{-1} g 3.6×10^{-4} h 5.7×10^{-5}
8. a 4.022 b 10.94 c 0.3628 d 1.469
   e 3.431 f 1.839 g 5.850 h -0.7379
9. a 9.77×10^0 b 4.29×10^1 c -4.29×10^1 d 5.50×10^2
   e 9.66×10^3 f 8.07×10^{-1} g 2.33×10^{-3} h 1.11×10^2
10. a 22 b -50 c 50 d -4
    e -216 f 0.8 g 1000 h 100
    i 0.01 j 1 k 10 000 l 10
11. a 0.190 b 0.422
12. a 0.4735 b 0.5641

Exercise 2 — page 6

1. 12
2. 8
3. £285 000
4. a 0.18p b 6 g
5. 450 km (approximately)
6. 201.6 kg
7. 10 litres
8. 64 years
9. 2×10^{-5} m

Exercise 3 — page 7

1. 3.75
2. 62.1
3. 69.6
4. 67.5%
5. 20%
6. 25%
7. 38.25 cm
8. 51.75 kg
9. 8%
10. 13.34 s
11. The tin is 454 g usually, therefore 68 g are 'free'.

Chapter 1 ARITHMETIC I

— Exercise 4 — page 8

1 **a** 678 900 **b** 0.0234
2 **a** [5.23 05] **b** [7.0301 09] **c** [3.15 −03] **d** [2.15 −06]
3 **a** 93.4 **b** 10.4 **c** $\sqrt{19} \times 89$
   d 1.989 [EXP] 5 [x^y] 5 [=]
   e 19 [x^2] [−] 89 [=]
   f [[(] 198 [−] 9 [x^2] [)]] [√]
   g 1.9 [EXP] 3 [×] 8.9 [EXP] 2 [=]
   h $(19 \times 10^8)^9$ **i** $(19 \times 10^{-8})^9$
   j [[(] 19 [x^y] 4 [−] 89 [x^2] [)]] [√] *or* 19 [x^y] 4 [−] 89 [x^y] 2 [=] [√]

4 6.5×10^8 5 4.5×10^3 6 1.9×10^5 7 1.6×10^{-9}
8 1.1×10^1 9 6.6×10^{-10} 10 1.7×10^3 11 4.0×10^5
12 1.2×10^3 13 1.73×10^9 14 6.2×10^{-5} 15 3.9×10^{17}
16 2.1×10^{-7} 17 5.1×10^{-18} 18 1.1×10^7 19 2.8×10^2
20 7.4×10^1

— Activity 1 — page 10

50, 51, 54, 52

— Activity 2 — page 10

Nina's profit = 80%. Matthew's profit = 8%. Nina appears to be ten times more successful.

— Exercise 5 — page 12

1 **a** 15% profit   **b** 18% profit   **c** £26.40   **d** 30% loss   **e** $83.70
   f £81.70   **g** $13.50   **h** £28   **i** 50% loss   **j** $19.71
   k £777.60   **l** 287.5 %
2 £244 200   3 £244 200 (4 SF)   4 £12 000
5 **a** 8.5%   **b** 15%   **c** 22%   **d** 48%
6 £60   7 £400
8 Retailer 45%, author 10%, distributor 5%, publisher 25%, printer 15%
9 216   10 £150   11 £2.98, £4.04, £5.25, £5.32, £6.92
12 £6.89   13 **a** (i) 69% (ii) 92% (iii) 72%   **b** 260%   **c** −   14 £462.86
15 £2.50   16 2p loss   17 20%   18 Rate of increase, decreases.

Activity 3 — page 14

Advertisements and financial sections of newspapers should provide a good source of material.

Exercise 6 — page 15

1 0.66 mph
2 26
3 £47.56
4 4120
5 1.37 cm
6 2.5×10^6
7 2×10^7
8 3×10^{10}
9 a 10^{10} b 1200 cm^2
10 $5.3 \times 10^5 \text{ m}^3$
11 2.03×10^{19} km
12 8.9×10^9
13 412.5 miles
14 a $3.7 billions   b $25.2 billions   c 12.5%
15 5 hours 40 minutes
16 a 6.6 kg/m^2 b 0.66 cm/day
17 a (i) 0.4 mm   (ii) 0.8 mm   (iii) 3.2 mm   (iv) 1.13×10^8 km
    b The last answer is approximately 293 times the distance to the Moon.
18 Assume 3 points for gold, 2 points for silver and 1 for bronze, in your investigation.

Country	Points	Points/M	Position
USSR	273	1.0	7th
E. Germany	211	12	1st
USA	197	0.87	8th
S. Korea	67	1.9	5th
W. Germany	76	1.3	6th
Hungary	51	5.0	3rd
Bulgaria	67	7.7	2nd
Romania	49	2.3	4th
France	32	0.61	10th
Italy	30	0.56	11th
China	49	0.050	12th
UK	44	0.74	9th

Revision Exercise 1 — page 18

1 a (i) 4.188   (ii) 24.12   (iii) 0.005 068   (iv) 1.709
   b (i) 1.26   (ii) 0.0220   (iii) 667   (iv) 2.15
2 a 1.28×10^9 km   b 71 minutes (approximately)
3 a 80%, 75%, 75%, 85%, 60%   b Pat, Steven, Mark and Anne (equal), Melissa
   c 112, last (same!)
4 a 26%   b £319   c £273.44
5 a £1344   b £1505.28   c £1685.91
6 a £176 profit   b 27.9%
7 a 70.0%   b 72.6%   c 30.1%   d 53.1%   e 53.7%
8 153 years
9 3.39×10^4 km since 1386
10 a 24.9 km/h   b 222 km/h   c 123 mph

Chapter 1 ARITHMETIC I

Basics Test 1   page 20

A Calculator
1 0.486
2 0.792
3 153
4 −0.003 96
5 33 400
6 1490

B Paper and pencil
7 0.13
8 $\frac{19}{30}$
9 437 cm²
10 £16.80
11 104 400
12 4.5 hours
13 £9.50
14 10 000 000
15 16.8 cm

C Mental
16 What is the total cost of two pints of lemonade? £1.80
17 What is the total cost of three packets of biscuits? £1.65
18 What is the cost of one pint of lemonade and one packet of biscuits? £1.45
19 What is the cost of two pints of lemonade and four packets of biscuits? £4.00
20 Jean buys six packets of biscuits. How much change should she get from five pounds? £1.70
21 Write down the number three million in standard form. 3×10^6
22 What is the square of point one? 0.01
23 Divide fifty six by point eight. 70
24 How many hours are there in eight days? 192
25 Multiply one third by one quarter. $\frac{1}{12}$

Puzzlers   page 20

1 Measure the thickness of, say 100 pages, and divide the measurement by 100.
2 11 of 1p, 20p, 50p and £1.
3 Backwards.

Chapter 1 ARITHMETIC I

— COURSEWORK: Kit Kar bars   page 21

MARKS (M) 4; (A) 5; (E) 4; (N) 2; (I) 2; (C) 3

Point out that more Kit Kat bars are sold each year than any other chocolate bar. Discuss different ways of comprehending the vast number sold. (Volume, mass, numbers sold per second, etc.) Discuss the degree of accuracy which is needed.

1 a Six ways are possible:

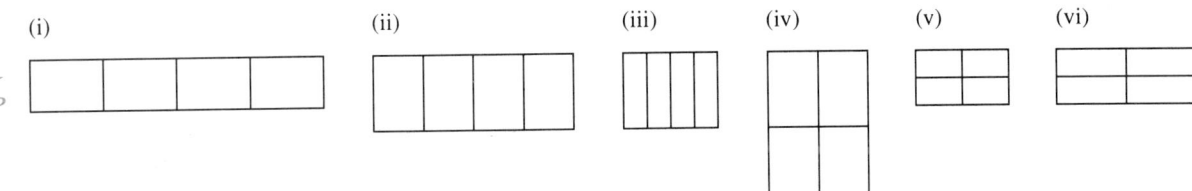

Pupils could discover how to use four books to help find these arrangements.
(iii), (v) and (vi) are the most compact and would therefore not be 'eyecatching' enough for a promotional packet. (i) would be more easily damaged than (iii) and (iv). (ii) would fit on the shelves more easily and is therefore the best arrangement.

b The promotional packet would give $33\frac{1}{3}\%$ more for the price.

2 Each bar measures 10.3 cm by 6.2 cm by 1.05 cm.

3 An arm span, for example, could be calibrated. The approximate number of boxes of 48 bars which can be fitted into the room could be calculated.

4 Total mass sold per year = $\frac{47.2 \times 1277 \times 10^6}{1000 \times 1000}$ tonnes.

Total mass is approximately equivalent to $\frac{60\,300}{375} \approx 160$ Jumbo jets.

5

	Day	Hour	Minute	Second
Mean number sold per	3.5 million	440 000	7300	120
Mean cost sold per	£870 000	£110 000	£1800	£30
Mean mass sold per	170 tonnes	21 tonnes	340 kg	5.7 kg

6 Total length of paper = $\frac{22.7 \times 1277 \times 10^6}{100 \times 1000}$ = 290 000 km correct to 2 SF.

Total length is approximately seven times the circumference of the Earth. However, with a 2 cm overlap per bar the total length is approximately eight times.

7 Total area of foil = $\frac{1277 \times 10^6 \times 178.607}{100^2 \times 1000^2}$ = 22.8 km² correct to 3 SF.

8 Calories/g, grams/p and perhaps calories/p could be worked out for a number of different chocolate bars. The proportion of bar which is not chocolate could also be considered. A survey could also be carried out.

Chapter 2 GRAPHS I

Exercise 7 — page 24

1. **a** For example, girl walking away from a fixed point at a constant speed.
   b For example, a car approaching a fixed point at a constant speed.
   c For example, a boat accelerates to reach a steady speed which it maintains before decelerating to a halt.
   d For example, diurnal temperature in London on 1st July.
2. **a** Graph (iii)   **b** Graph (i)   **c** Graph (iii)   **d** Graph (i)
   (The meaning of all the graphs should be discussed.)

3.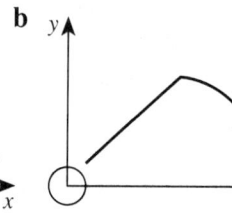
4.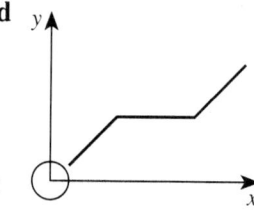

5.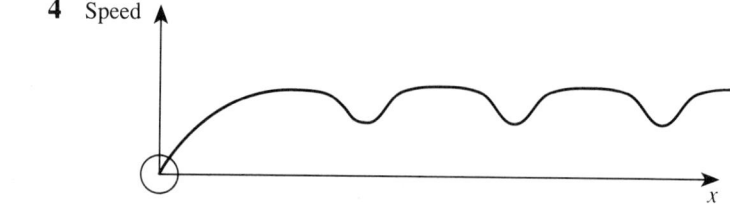

6. **a** Graph I: B   **b** Graph II: C   **c** Graph III: A

Exercise 8 — page 27

1. **a** Penny   **b** 1st April, 1st September   **c** $\frac{5}{8}$ kg per month   **d** January to July
   e January   **f** June
2. **a** UK population of 21–24 year olds between 1980 and 2000.
   b A slight recovery, levelling off: any **sensible** answer.
   d (i) 3.1 million to 3.7 million: 19% increase.   (ii) 3.7 million to 2.6 million: 30% decrease.
   e The decrease might be due to more working women and better contraception, etc.
3. **a** 4 minutes 4 seconds   **b** 48.5 seconds   **c** Female by 3 seconds (23.3 m)
4. **a** Petrol tank being filled   **b** 6 gallons   **c** (i) 40 mpg   (ii) 25 mpg
   d 'Motorway driving' is before the first stop as consumption of fuel per mile is less.
   e 30 mpg   **f** Four gallons remain.

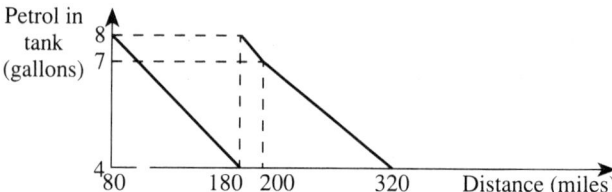

Chapter 2 GRAPHS I

5 **a** 4800 vehicles/h   **b** 20 mph and 44 mph   **c** 32 mph
   d 70 mph. Greater speed, therefore distance between vehicles is greater!
   e 52 m   **f** 4.5 m, approximately 6000 vehicles/h

Exercise 9   page 29

1

Side of square (cm)	0	2	4	6	8	10
Area of square (cm²)	0	4	16	36	64	100

  b (i) 30.25 cm² (ii) 7.42 cm

2 **a** (i) 6 m (ii) 14 m
   b

Width (m)	1	1.5	2	3	4	5	6
Height (m)	6	4	3	2	1.5	1.2	1
Perimeter (m)	14	11	10	10	11	12.4	14

   d Perimeter = 9.8 m: 2.45 m × 2.45 m   **e** £294

3 **a**

Number of days digging	0	1	2	3	4
Tunnel length dug (m)	0	17	30	37	42

   c 5.7 days   **d** £142 500

4 **a** 86.6 m   **b**

Angle of depression	30°	40°	45°	50°	60°	70°	80°	90°
Distance from harbour (m)	87	60	50	42	29	18	8.8	0

   d 35.5°
   e 14.3 seconds. The ship may not have been on a course at right angles to the cliff.

5

Speed (m/s)	0	10	15.6	20	26.8	50
Speed (mph)	0	22.4	35	44.7	60	111.9

   b (i) 11.2 mph   (ii) 22.3 m/s
   c Downhill skier: 22.3 m/s   Racehorse: 19.6 m/s
          Killer whale: 14.3 m/s   Cyclist: 13.4 m/s
          Olympic athlete: 5.6 m/s   Olympic swimmer: 2.1 m/s
   d x m/s $= \frac{x}{1609} \times 60 \times 60$ mph $= 2.237x$ mph $= v$

Chapter 2 GRAPHS I

Exercise 10 — page 33

1. **a** 09:30 for half an hour **b** 40 mph **c** 09:00 and 10:54 **d** 20 miles **e** 80 mph. Yes! **f** Excluding stops: 53.3 mph for both.

2. **a**

   (Distance–time graph: from 09:00 rises to 60 km at 10:15, to 80 km at 11:15, stays at 80 km until 13:00, then decreases to 0 by 14:00.)

   b 14:00 hours

3. **a** (i) B and C joint 1st, A 2nd (ii) C 1st, B 2nd, A 3rd (iii) A 1st, B 2nd, C 3rd
   b 28.5 seconds **c** B **d** A **e** C

4. **a**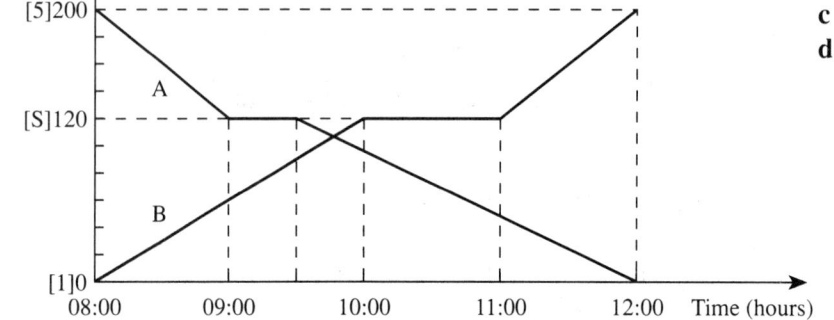

   b 09:47 **c** 48 km/h **d** 80 km/h

   e Driver A = 57 km/h (2 SF) excluding stops. Driver B = 67 km/h (2 SF) excluding stops.

Exercise 11 — page 35

1. **a** 2 m/s^2 **b** -4 m/s^2 **c** 150 m **d** 10 m/s
2. **a** 3.5 km/h^2 **b** -7 km/h^2 **c** 10.5 km **d** 3.5 km/h
3. **a** $S = 120$ m/s **b** 9600 m **c** 80 m/s
4. **a** 30 m/s **b** 10 seconds **c** 570 ± 15 m **d** 22.8 ± 0.6 m/s
5. **a** $t = 10$ seconds therefore distance = 1900 m **b** -3 m/s^2 **c** 47.5 m/s

Revision Exercise 2 — page 37

1. A 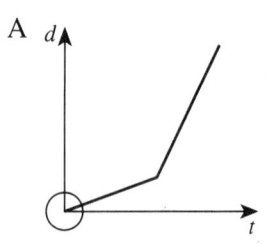 B 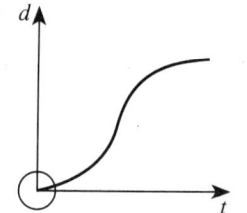 C 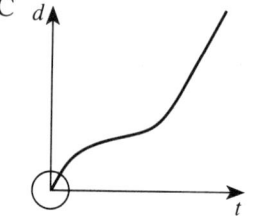 D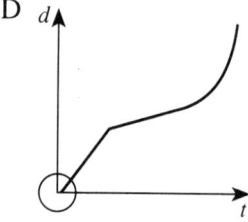

Chapter 2 GRAPHS I

2 **a**  **b** 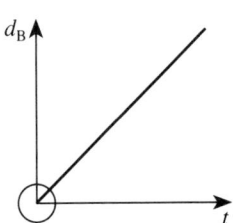 **c** 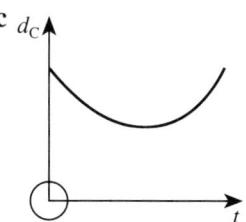 **d**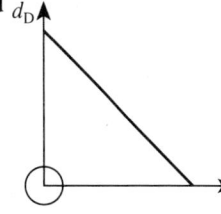

3 **a** (i) 10.5 km/ℓ (ii) 3 gallons
b 28 mpg
c The cars are travelling at different speeds so their consumptions are not comparable.

4 **a**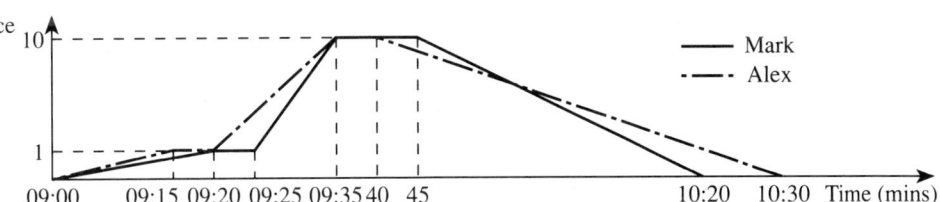

b (i) Mark at 10:20, Alex at 10:30.
(ii) Mark and Alex are equal at 09:20, 09:35–09:40 and 09:57.
c Mark: 18.5 km/h   Alex: 15 km/h

5 **a**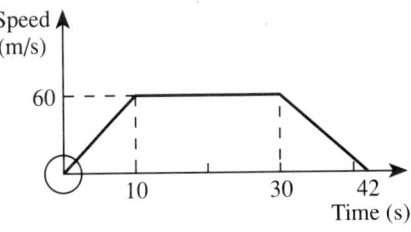

b (i) 0.6 m/s^2 (ii) -0.5 m/s^2 (iii) 4.4 m/s

6 **a**

	Hare	Dog	Man	Horse
Pulse (Beats/min)	200	135	83	65
Mass (kg)	3	12	70	200

b (i) Total heartbeats for human of life-span 75 years = 3.27×10^9
(ii) According to the 'fringe' theory:

	Hare	Dog	Man	Horse
Lifespan (years)	31.1	46.1	75	95.8

Clearly, from these figures, the 'fringe' theory is not correct.

17

Chapter 2 GRAPHS I

___ Basic Algebra Test 1   page 39

1 $2a$	**2** a^2	**3** $2e$	**4** 8
5 $d+e$	**6** $2d^2e$	**7** x^2	**8** $2x^3$
9 $3-x$	**10** $3x$	**11** $\frac{1}{3}$	**12** 3
13 -4	**14** 3	**15** -6	**16** 2
17 6	**18** 27	**19** 7	**20** 6
21 $3(x+1)$	**22** $x(4-x)$	**23** $x > \frac{3}{5}$	**24** $y \leq 2$
25 $\frac{7x}{15}$	**26** $\frac{x^2}{9}$	**27** $\frac{x^3}{9}$	**28** $11c^2$
29 8	**30** $2\frac{1}{2}$	**31** $-\frac{3}{4}$	**32** $\frac{6}{11}$

___ Puzzlers   page 39

1 Pupils should estimate the average number of words per line from about ten randomly selected lines. They should then multiply this by the average number of lines per page and by the number of pages in the book.

2 SEND = 9567, MORE = 1085, MONEY = 10652

3 e Quince, quance, quonce. (35 quince = 20 quonce = 24 quance.)

Chapter 2 GRAPHS I

COURSEWORK: World sprint record — page 40

MARKS (M) 3; (A) 5; (E) 4; (N) 3; (I) 2; (C) 3

Pupils are expected to realise that the finishing times of the sprinters occur when their chests cross the finishing line.

1

Competitor	Finishing time (s)	d (m)
Johnson	9.83	–
Lewis	9.93	1.01
Stewart	10.08	2.48
Christie	10.14	3.06

2 a Look for accurate plotting and sensible choice of scale.
  b Each pupil's 200 m time is not the same multiple of his 100 m time. 'Alien' points could be due to tiredness, not sprinting 'flat out' for both distances.
  c Look for calculations using tabulation. Ensure 'best time' goes through M.

3 a Use of $d = 100(1 - \frac{9.83}{t})$ metres.
  b Use of 'best' straight line should be shown.

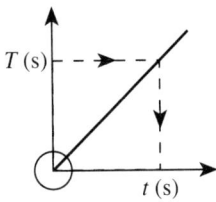

4 d = 100 − distance travelled in 9.83 seconds
   = 100 − (pupil's speed) × 9.83
   = 100 − $\frac{100}{t}$ × 9.83
Therefore $d = 100(1 - \frac{9.83}{t})$ m

5 a At no time should the pupil's curve cross Johnson's or be steeper.
   b At no time should the pupil's curve cross Johnson's.

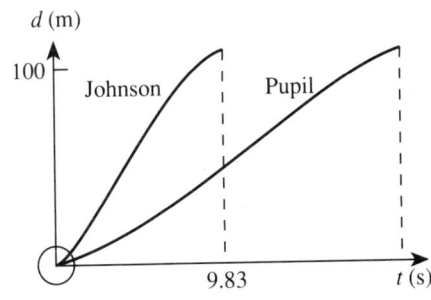
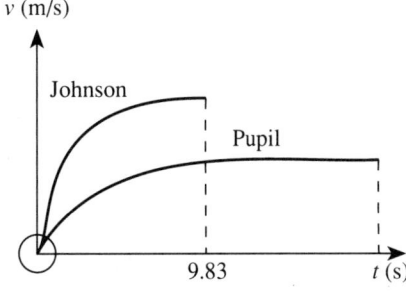

An explanation of each curve and an attempt at calibrating each vertical axis would gain marks for initiative.

Chapter 3 ALGEBRA I

Exercise 12 — page 43

1. **a** $2b^2$ **b** $3b$ **c** 2 **d** $8a^2$ **e** $2a$
   f 2 **g** $\frac{c}{3}$ **h** 4 **i** $4a^2$ **j** $8a^3$
2. **a** -1 **b** 40 **c** -2 **d** -2 **e** -6
   f 1 **g** 1600 **h** 12 **i** 1 **j** 45
3. **a** $2(x+1)$ **b** $x(3x+1)$ **c** $x(y+2)$ **d** $2y(x-2z)$ **e** $2x(x-2)$
   f $4b(3+a)$ **g** $ab(b-3c)$ **h** $ab(3c-b)$ **i** $3a(a-4)$ **j** $3a^2(a-4)$
4. **a** $a = 18$ **b** $a = 7.9$ **c** $a = 2$ **d** $a = 7$
5. **a** $b = 11$ **b** $b = 4.4$ **c** $b = 8$ **d** $b = 9$
6. **a** $c = -1$ **b** $c = 8.1$ **c** $c = 1$ **d** $c = 3$
7. **a** $d = 25$ **b** $d = 110$ **c** $d = 16$ **d** $d = 125$
8. **a** $e = 47$ **b** $e = 4.2$ **c** $e = 11$ **d** $e = 6$
9. **a** $f = 3$ **b** $f = 12.5$ **c** $f = 130$ **d** $f = 8$
10. **a** $g = 2$ **b** $g = 1$ **c** $g = -2$ **d** $g = \frac{1}{3}$

Exercise 13 — page 45

1.

	Term number (n)				Rule for nth term
	1	2	3	4	
a	6	12	18	24	**$6n$**
b	6	7	8	9	**$n + 5$**
c	4	8	12	16	$4n$
d	8	9	10	11	$n + 7$
e	19	18	17	16	**$20 - n$**
f	-2	-1	0	1	**$n - 3$**
g	7	11	15	19	$4n + 3$
h	4	9	14	19	**$5n - 1$**
i	3	6	11	18	$n^2 + 2$
j	1.5	3	5.5	9	$\frac{n^2 + 2}{2}$

2.

Number of circles (n)	1	2	3	4	5	6
Number of dots	0	2	4	6	8	10

b $2n - 2$ **c** 1498 **d** 501

3. Rule: $4n + 1$, 50th cross contains 201 squares.

Exercise 14 — page 46

1. $x = -1$ 2. $y = -1\frac{1}{4}$ 3. $z = \frac{1}{2}$ 4. $p = 1$ 5. $a = \frac{5}{12}$
6. $b = 2\frac{1}{4}$ 7. $c = -1\frac{1}{4}$ 8. $d = \frac{1}{3}$ 9. $t = -11$ 10. $w = -17$

Chapter 3 ALGEBRA I

Exercise 15 — page 48

1. **a** $10q$ **b** $24k$ **c** $\frac{d}{12}$ **d** $d+e$ **e** yx
2. 5.3 miles
3. 0.39 s (2 SF)
4. 18.4 m
5. 8 cm
6. $x = 9$ cm
7. $x = 3.2$ cm

Exercise 16 — page 51

1. 25, 26, 27
2. 18, 19, 20, 21
3. 37, 38, 39
4. 13
5. 7.5
6. 8
7. 72
8. 13 cm
9. 52 m, 46 m
10. 13, 27
11. 6 years
12. David 17 years, Tariq 14 years, Carl 9 years
13. Ann 55 kg, Linda 48 kg, Justine 64 kg
14. Sweater = £29.50
15. $x = 4$ cm. Area = $7 \times 14 = 98$ cm^2
16. **a** $65x$ km **b** $1.2t$ hours **c** $\frac{65x}{1.2t}$ km/h

Exercise 17 — page 52

1. $\frac{3}{10}$
2. $\frac{a^2}{2}$
3. $2b$
4. $\frac{a^3c^2}{b}$
5. $3\frac{3}{8}$
6. $\frac{4}{5}$
7. $\frac{b^2}{c}$
8. $\frac{3ab^4}{c^2}$
9. $1\frac{3}{20}$
10. $\frac{11a}{12}$
11. $1\frac{14}{15}a$
12. $\frac{5a+2}{6}$
13. $\frac{1}{2}$
14. $\frac{7a}{15}$
15. $\frac{ad-bc}{bd}$
16. $\frac{a-6}{4}$
17. $\frac{11}{3a}$
18. $\frac{9a+2}{6}$
19. $\frac{5-5a}{6}$
20. $\frac{a-10}{12}$
21. $\frac{2b}{3}$
22. $\frac{2ac}{b}$
23. $2a^2$
24. $\frac{6ab}{c}$
25. $9-a$
26. $1 + \frac{3a}{2}$ or $1 + 1\frac{1}{2}a$
27. $\frac{1}{3b} + \frac{2}{3a}$
28. $a - 2$
29. $\frac{5(a+1)}{(a+3)(a-2)}$
30. $\frac{a+7}{(2a-1)(3a+1)}$

Exercise 18 — page 54

1. $x = 6$
2. $x = 60$
3. $x = 2\frac{1}{2}$
4. $x = -\frac{3}{7}$
5. $x = 20$
6. $x = -7\frac{1}{2}$
7. $x = -2$
8. $x = -\frac{4}{5}$
9. $x = -6$
10. $x = -7$
11. $x = 7\frac{1}{5}$
12. $x = 12$
13. $x = -3$
14. $x = -15$
15. $x = -4\frac{2}{7}$
16. $x = \frac{5}{13}$
17. $x = 15\frac{2}{3}$
18. $x = -\frac{1}{4}$
19. $x = -\frac{3}{7}$
20. $x = -5\frac{2}{9}$
21. $x = -1\frac{5}{9}$
22. $x = \frac{19}{27}$
23. $x = -\frac{7}{8}$
24. $x = -\frac{19}{22}$
25. $x = -3\frac{4}{11}$

Chapter 3 ALGEBRA I

── Exercise 19   page 55

1. $x = 1$, $y = 2$
2. $x = 2$, $y = 5$
3. $x = 4$, $y = 11$
4. $x = 6$, $y = 31$
5. $x = 2.5$, $y = 13$
6. $x = 1.5$, $y = 4$
7. $x = -2$, $y = 16$
8. $x = -1.5$, $y = 4$
9. $x = 7$, $y = 21$
10. $x = -12$, $y = 2$
11. $x = 3$, $y = -4$
12. $x = -0.5$, $y = -4$

── Exercise 20   page 57

1. **a** $-3 > -6$ **b** $-8 < 1$ **c** $0.15 < \frac{1}{6}$ **d** $\pi^2 < 10$
2. **a** $x > 4$ **b** $x \geqslant 6$ **c** $x \geqslant 3$ **d** $x < 1$
3. **a** $x \geqslant 4$, $\{4, 5, 6\}$ **b** $x < 27$, $\{26, 25, 24\}$
   c $x > 9$, $\{10, 11, 12\}$ **d** $x \geqslant 9$, $\{9, 10, 11\}$
4. **a** $-1 \leqslant x < 4$ **b** $-3 < x \leqslant 1$ **c** $-5 < x \leqslant 8$ **d** $x < 7$

── Revision Exercise 3   page 58

1. **a** $3a - 3b - 4$ **b** $4xy - 2x$ **c** y^6 **d** $8pq + 2p^2 - q^2$
   e 4 **f** $32y^5$
2. **a** $x + 3$ **b** $11 - 2y$ **c** $5p - 1$ **d** $2x^2 - xy$
   e $3a - 5$ **f** $8x^2 + 3x - 8$
3. **a** 11 **b** -18 **c** 29 **d** $\frac{1}{2}$
   e 2 **f** 0
4. **a** 3.0×10^1 **b** 3.1×10^{-4} **c** 6.3×10^{-4} **d** 4.7×10^{-4}
   e 5.3×10^{-2} **f** 2.2×10^2
5. **a** $a(b + c) = -1$ **b** $(a + b)c^2 = 27$ **c** $3(b^2 + a) = 15$ **d** $ab(c + a) = -4$
   e $2(b - a)c^2 = 18$ **f** $(3a - c)b^2 = 24$
6. **a** $2(x + 3y)$ **b** $x(y - 3)$ **c** $pq(q - 2)$ **d** $4a(b - 2a)$
   e $uv(u - v)$ **f** $2ab(b + 3a)$
7. **a** $p = 7$ **b** $p = -4$ **c** $q = 75$ **d** $q = 15$
   e $r = \frac{3}{8}$ **f** $r = \frac{1}{2}$
8. **a** $a = \frac{1}{3}$ **b** $a = -1\frac{1}{2}$ **c** $x = \frac{1}{4}$ **d** $x = 1$
   e $t = -1$ **f** $t = \frac{1}{18}$
9. **a** $w = 1\frac{1}{2}$ **b** $w = 9$ **c** $a = -4$ **d** $a = -\frac{1}{3}$
   e $e = -1\frac{2}{5}$ **f** $e = \frac{1}{20}$
10. $z = 22°$
11. 9 cm
12. $30°, 60°, 90°$
13. $x = 3$, $y = -1$
14. $11, 13, 15$
15. 5
16. Alice: 13 years, Rupinder: 9 years, Julia: 6 years
17. **a** $x > 3$ **b** $x \geqslant 5$ **c** $x \leqslant 5$ **d** $x < \frac{2}{5}$ **e** $x \geqslant 1\frac{1}{5}$ **f** $x < 2$
18. **a** $\frac{2a - b}{2a - 4b}$ **b** $\frac{cd - ab}{bd + ac}$
19. **a** $x = -2\frac{1}{17}$ **b** $x = 5\frac{4}{7}$
20. 16 km
21. **a** $xy = -2\frac{1}{2}$ **b** $mn = \frac{2}{3}$
22. 12 m^2

Chapter 3 ALGEBRA I

▭ Aural Test 1   page 60

1	Fifty envelopes cost ninety pence. How much do one hundred and fifty cost?	£2.70
2	How many square millimetres are there in two square centimetres?	200
3	Jane gets nine out of twenty in a test. What percentage is this?	45%
4	One pound can be exchanged for twelve francs. How many pounds can be exchanged for seventy two francs?	6
5	A road is eight kilometres long. How long is it in miles, approximately?	5 miles
6	Two angles of a triangle are forty three and sixty nine degrees. What is the size of the third angle?	68°
7	A radio programme begins at 10:52 and finishes at 12:16. How many minutes does it last?	84 minutes
8	A book is bought for £25 and sold at a loss of 22%. For how much was it sold?	£19.50
9	Write down the number point nought nine four eight correct to one significant figure.	0.09
10	When a equals minus 3, what is the value of two a squared?	18
11	The diagram represents the dials on a gas metre which measures units of gas. How many whole units are shown?	2494
12	The previous reading was 2131. How many units have been used since the previous reading?	363
13	Which of the answers shown is the approximate answer to the multiplication three times five point eight times thirty two?	c: 560
14	Which of the lengths shown is approximately two thirds of a mile?	c: 1000 m
15	What is the total charge for two adults and three children?	£6.30
16	What is the maximum number of people that could be admitted for ten pounds?	11 children
17	What change should be given from twenty pounds for the admission of six adults and four children?	£5.60
18	ABCD is a parallelogram. What is the side length AB?	7.8 cm
19	What is the size of angle ADC?	68°
20	John's basic rate of pay is three pounds per hour. He is paid four pounds per hour for overtime. What is his total pay for the week?	£146

▭ Puzzler   page 60

Assuming that **all** the money (3600 crowns) will be available as he has a son **and** a daughter, and that each pair will have the same ratio of money as stated in the will (ie, daughter to wife; son to wife).

$$\begin{array}{cc} Daughter & Wife \\ \dfrac{2}{6} & \dfrac{3}{6} \end{array} \qquad \begin{array}{cc} Son & Wife \\ \dfrac{3}{6} & \dfrac{2}{6} \end{array}$$

Therefore son : wife : daughter = 9 : 6 : 4
Therefore son : wife : daughter = $1705\frac{5}{19}$ crowns : $1136\frac{16}{19}$ crowns : $757\frac{17}{19}$ crowns

COURSEWORK: Motoring costs page 61

MARKS (M) 3; (A) 5; (E) 4; (N) 3; (I) 2; (C) 3

This Coursework should make pupils more aware of the real costs of motoring. Stress the importance of reading the details carefully and not jumping to conclusions. Check that each pupil has labelled and calibrated each of the 5 graphs correctly **before** completing the table of information.

1 and 2 a Fuel: apart from year 3 there is little variation in the cost each year. 1 unit = £50.

    b Insurance: it is the only cost which is likely to be reduced each successive year. 1 unit = £50.

    c Road Tax: this rarely changes from one year to the next, but in Rachel's case it did increase by £20 after she had been driving her sports car for three years. 1 unit = £10.

    d Maintenance: this cost is likely to increase as the car increases in age. 1 unit = £45. This is worked out by dividing the total height of the five bars (20 units) into £900.

    e Depreciation: it is the only graph to show a decrease in each successive year. 1 unit = £1000.

3 a

Year	Annual cost (£)				
	Maintenance	Road tax	Depreciation	Insurance	Fuel
1	45	80	3000	550	300
2	90	80	2000	450	250
3	135	80	1000	400	500
4	270	100	500	350	300
5	360	100	500	350	250

  b Average total cost per week = $\frac{12\,040}{260}$ = £46.31.

4 The fuel tank should be completely filled and the mileometer put back to zero. At the next visit to a garage the tank is again completely filled and the amount of fuel put in is noted, together with the distance on the mileometer.

5 Total fuel cost over 5 years = £1600.   Fuel consumption is 36 mpg.
Cost of petrol is £2.50/gallon.   Number of gallons = £$\frac{1600}{2.50}$ = 640
Mileage = 640 × 36 = 23 040   Cost/mile = £$\frac{12040}{23040}$ = £0.52/mile.

6 Total **interest** repaid to bank over five years = £9900 − £7000 = £2900
Total **interest** repaid to HP company over five years = £14 400 − £7000 = £7400.

	Total cost/mile	Total cost/week
Bank	$\frac{12\,040+2900}{230\,40}$ = £0.65	$\frac{12\,040+2900}{260}$ = £57.46
HP	$\frac{12\,040+7400}{230\,40}$ = £0.84	$\frac{12\,040+7400}{260}$ = £74.77

The HP figures are approximately 30% more than the bank figures. (The interest repayments would have been more because the cost of the car was £10 000 and not £7000.) Pupils could obtain details of other interest rates.

Chapter 3 ALGEBRA I

FACT FINDERS: The UK hurricane — page 62

1. Previous storm = current year − 1703

2. In 1 hour the wind travelled 97 miles.
   In 1 second the wind travelled $\frac{97 \times 1600}{3600}$ = 43.1 metres to 3 SF.
   Therefore wind speed = 43.1 metres/second.

3. Rate of increase = $\frac{1004 - 959}{5}$ = 9 millibars/hour

4. Percentage of homes without electricity = $\frac{3 \text{ million}}{22 \text{ million}} \times 100$ = 13.6%

5. Volume of wood = 9 × 15 million = 1.35×10^8 m³

6. Poles/minute = $\frac{3000}{5 \times 60}$ = 10

7. Premium paid in 1987 = $230 \times \frac{100}{115}$ = £200

8. Total sales = (£4.75 × 25 000) + £$\left(\frac{2.25 \times 25\,000}{12}\right)$ = 123 437.50

9. Mean speed = $\frac{432 \times 10^3}{1600} \div 5$ = 54 mph

10. Minimum hurricane wind speed = $\frac{32.7 \times 3600}{1600} \approx$ 73.6 mph
    Other wind speeds could also be investigated.

Chapter 4 GEOMETRY I

Exercise 21 — page 66

1. $a = 70°$, $b = 40°$
2. $a = 36°$, $b = 144°$
3. $a = 34°$, $b = 56°$
4. $a = 39°$, $b = 51°$
5. $a = 40°$, $b = 70°$
6. $a = 50°$, $b = 45°$
7. $a = 105°$, $b = 20°$
8. $a = 56°$, $b = 34°$
9. $a = 49°$, $b = 82°$
10. $a = 120°$, $b = 60°$
11. $a = 38°$, $b = 56°$
12. $a = 105°$, $b = 25°$
13. $a = 108°$, $b = 36°$, $c = 36°$, $d = 108°$
14. Angle ADB = 116° (Angles at a point) Angle DBC = 26° (Isosceles triangle)
    Angle ABD = 26° (Angle sum of triangle) Angle ACB = 52° (AD is axis of symmetry)
15. Angle ADE = 62° (Isosceles trapezium) Angle AED = 77° (Angle sum of triangle)
    Angle BEC = 49° (Angles on a straight line) Angle EAB = 77° (Alternate angles)
16. Angle CDE = 135° (Regular octagon) Angle ABG = 45° (ABGH isosceles trapezium)
    Angle BFE = $67\frac{1}{2}°$ (Angle sum of triangle) Angle FBG = $22\frac{1}{2}°$ (Angle sum of triangle)
17. Angle ABC = 48° (Angle of parallelogram) Angle ADC = 48° (Opposite angles of parallelogram)
    Angle ADE = 24° (Angles on straight line) Angle AED = 108° (Corresponding)

Activity 5 — page 67

All the angles formed at the circumference of a circle off its diameter are right angles.

Activity 6 — page 67

The angle between the tangent of a circle to the radius of the circle from the point of contact of the tangent is also a right angle.

Exercise 22 — page 68

1. $a = 90°$, $b = 90°$, $c = 25°$
2. $a = 90°$, $b = 30°$, $c = 30°$
3. $a = 90°$, $b = 58°$, $c = 50°$
4. $a = 45°$, $b = 45°$, $c = 53°$
5. $a = 104°$, $b = 76°$, $c = 52°$
6. $a = 90°$, $b = 18°$, $c = 72°$
7. $a = 45°$, $b = 45°$, $c = 90°$
8. $a = 132°$, $b = 24°$, $c = 66°$
9. $a = 32°$, $b = 132°$, $c = 80°$
10. $a = 62°$, $b = 28°$, $c = 124°$
11. $a = 46°$, $b = 88°$, $c = 46°$
12. $a = 36°$, $b = 54°$, $c = 108°$
13. Angle ABE = 54°, angle BED = 54°. AB parallel to CD.
14. Angle ACD = 37°, angle BCX = 53°. Right-angled kite
15. Right-angled kite, isosceles trapezium, square, rectangle
16. Angle FBG = 126°, angle GCH = 54°. Isosceles trapezium
17. Angle ADE = 127°, angle ECF = 53°. Parallelogram (rhombus)
18. Angle OBE = 20°, angle OEB = 20°, angle BOE = 140°, angle BOD = 40°, angle OBD = 70°, angle ODB = 70°, angle BDC = 110°, angle DBC = 20°, angle OCB = 50°, angle OBC = 90°
20. Angle ABO = x, angle AOB = $180 - 2x$, angle ABD = $90 - x$
21. Angle CAD = $90 - x$ = angle BCA, angle BCD = 90°
22. Angle OBA = $90 - x$, angle AOB = $2x$, angle COB = $180 - 2x$

Chapter 4 GEOMETRY I

23 Angle BCA = $90 + x$, angle ABC = $90 - 2x$, angle BOC = $2x$
24 Angle OAC = $\frac{180-x}{2}$, angle OBC = $\frac{x}{2}$, angle ACB = $90°$
25 Angle COB = $180 - 2x$, angle BOA = $\frac{x}{2}$, angle AOC = $180 - 1\frac{1}{2}x$

___ Activity 7 — page 70

1 △ ABC 40°, 60°, 80°   △ DEF 40°, 60°, 80°   △ GHI 40°, 70°, 70°
2 $\frac{AC}{DF} = \frac{AB}{DE} = \frac{BC}{EF} \approx 0.79$ $\frac{AB}{GH} \approx 0.73$ $\frac{AC}{GI} \approx 0.65$ $\frac{EF}{HI} \approx 0.89$

___ Exercise 23 — page 71

1 a and b   2 a and c   3 a and b   4 a and c   5 b and c

___ Activity 8 — page 72

Angle BRA = angle XRY (angle of reflection = angle of incidence)
BA and XY are vertical.

___ Exercise 24 — page 73

1 AC = 4 cm   2 XZ = 7.5 cm   3 HK = 3 cm   4 DE = 7.2 cm
5 XY = 2.4 cm   6 LM = 5.5 cm   7 OP = 42 cm   8 AC = 6.8 cm
9 BD = 3 m   10 EC = 9 m therefore ED = 3 m
11 AE = 7.5 m   12 Height = 19.6 m   13 Shadow = 1.6 m   14 a, d, e
15 No   16 a   17 b   18 BE = 2.25 cm
19 AD = 8 cm   20 Shadow = 5.5 m   21 135°

___ Exercise 25 — page 77

1 a 3   b 0.008   c 0.6̇   d 0.04
2 7.5 m   3 4.9 m   4 3.5 m   5 2.4 m
6 2 m   7 b   8 279 m + 161 m + 240 m = 680 m
9 Gradients: AB: 0.33, BC: 0.71, CD: 0.50, DE: 1.0, EF: 0.67, FG: 1.67,
   GH: 1.25, HI: 1.7
10 The two sloping roofs meet at 90°.

Chapter 4 GEOMETRY I

Revision Exercise 4 — page 79

1. **a** $a = 60°$, $b = 60°$, $c = 100°$ **b** $a = 70°$, $b = 49°$, $c = 131°$
   c $a = 116°$, $b = 32°$, $c = 32°$ **d** $a = 120°$, $b = 110°$, $c = 60°$
2. **a** $60°$ **b** $45°$ **c** $18°$ **d** $\frac{360}{n}°$
3. **a** $a = 41°$, $b = 98°$, $c = 82°$ **b** $a = 90°$, $b = 50°$, $c = 50°$, $d = 80°$
   c $a = 90°$, $b = 28°$, $c = 62°$ **d** $a = 134°$, $b = 23°$, $c = 67°$
4. **a** $a = 4$ **b** $x = 9.6$, $y = 2.4$ **c** $c = 5$ **d** $x = 3$, $y = 6$, $z = 3.6$
5. Gradients to 3 SF: **a** 0.333   **b** 0.250   **c** 0.171   **d** 0.167. Therefore **b**, **c** or **d**.
6. **a** Gradients to 3 SF: (i) AB: 0.200   (ii) BC: 1.25   (iii) CD: 0.909   **b** 0.531 to 3 SF
7. **b** Gradients to 3 SF: (i) AB: 0.500, BC: 1.10, CD: 1.25, DE: 0.21
   (ii) AQ: 1.00, QR: 1.25, RS: 1.00, ST: 0.625
8. Angle AXZ = 30° (triangle WXA is isosceles)
9. 2.4 m
10. **a** 10   **b** 12   **c** 15   **d** $\left(\frac{360}{180-x}\right)°$

Basics Test 2 — page 81

A Calculator
1. 0.383
2. 0.00110
3. 8800
4. 8.88
5. 1.54
6. −2.73

B Paper and pencil
7. 0.4
8. $8\frac{1}{4}$
9. 36 cm²
10. 7
11. 1 690 000
12. $\frac{47}{60}$
13. £137 500
14. 0.008 mm
15. 58 kg

C Mental
16. What is the value of bd?   −12
17. What is the value of c minus a?   2
18. What is the value of d times b squared?   36
19. What is the value of db all squared?   144
20. What is the value of $abcd$?   0
21. Multiply nine by six hundred.   5400
22. Divide seventy two by one point two.   60
23. What is five per cent of five thousand?   250
24. Write twenty four million in standard form. 2.4×10^7
25. What is the square root of two hundred and twenty five?   15

Chapter 4 GEOMETRY I

___ Puzzlers   page 81

1   The time it takes a car to travel a measured distance is used to calculate the speed of the car in mph. A conversion graph could be drawn.
    An alternative method is to time how long it takes a car to pass a certain window (see diagram).

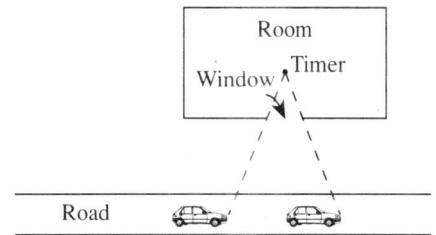

2   THING = 16043, H = 6, SHAWL = 96258
    or THING = 16057, H = 6, SHAWL = 96342

3   The left-hand wheel rotates 16 times per minute. The smallest wheel rotates 60 times per minute. Therefore its diameter is 8 cm.

___ COURSEWORK: The Cross-staff   page 82

MARKS (M) 2;   (A) 4;   (E) 5;   (N) 4;   (I) 2;   (C) 3

This is an interesting and practical way of using similar triangles. The Cross-staff was devised in the sixteenth century to estimate the width of a building or an advancing army from a distance.

1   Assuming that XY is parallel to AB, then triangles ABP and XYP are similar.
    Therefore $\frac{AB}{24} = \frac{2500}{20}$
    Therefore AB = 30 m.

2   A brief description of how the home-made Cross-staff is used should be included, together with any points affecting its accuracy. (Ruler placed at right angles to the metre rule, metre rule pointed to the mid point of the building and at right angles to it, metre rule bisects ruler.)
    Diagram, calculation, percentage error.

3   Description of how to use it, diagram, table of measurements.
    c d Check that XY + PZ = P'Z'.
    e The distance P'P should be the same in each case and this distance corresponds to the width of the building. (Some pupils may find it necessary to first measure the building with a tape measure.)

4   a A number of different possibilities could be considered:
       (i) The metre rule pointed horizontally to a point half way up the building would work but is not practical.
       (ii) The metre rule placed on the ground with the ruler held vertically would also work, but is not very practical.
       (iii) The diagram shows the best method. However, the metre rule must be held horizontally and the ruler held vertically.

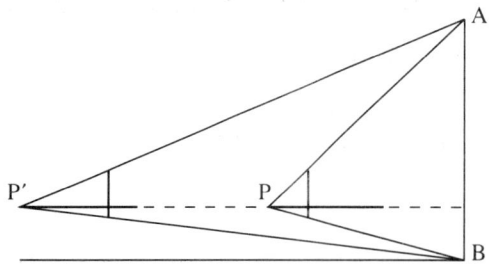

b $\frac{AB}{XY} = \frac{PD}{PZ}$, therefore $AB = \frac{2000}{40} \times 30 = 1500$ cm

$P'Z' = 30 + 40 = 70$ cm

$\frac{DP'}{Z'P'} = \frac{AB}{X'Y'}$, therefore $DP' = \frac{1500}{30} \times 70 = 3500$ cm

$PP' = DP' - DP = 3500 - 2000 = 1500$ cm

c $\frac{AB}{XY} = \frac{PD}{PZ}$, therefore $AB = \frac{q}{20} \times 30 = 1.5q$

$\frac{DP'}{Z'P'} = \frac{AB}{X'Y'}$, therefore $DP' = \frac{1.5q}{30} \times 50 = 2.5q$

$PP' = DP' - DP = 2.5q - q = 1.5q$

In **b** and **c**, $AB = PP'$

d $\frac{AB}{XY} = \frac{PD}{PZ}$, therefore $AB = x = \frac{cq}{a}$

$\frac{DP'}{Z'P'} = \frac{AB}{X'Y'}$, therefore $DP' = AB \times \frac{Z'P'}{X'Y'} = \frac{cq}{a} \times \frac{b}{c} = \frac{bq}{a}$

$PP' = DP' - DP$, therefore $y = \frac{bq}{a} - q = \frac{bq - aq}{a} = \frac{q(b-a)}{a}$

But $(b - a) = c$, therefore $y = \frac{cq}{a}$

Therefore $AB = PP'$

MULTIPLE CHOICE TEST 1A — page 242

For Chapters 1 to 4.

1 c	2 d	3 c	4 a	5 d	6 b	7 d	8 c	9 d	10 c	
11 a	12 c	13 b (56.1%)	14 a	15 b	16 d	17 d	18 c	19 a	20 d

MULTIPLE CHOICE TEST 1B — page 244

For Chapters 1 to 4.

1 b	2 d	3 a	4 d	5 a	6 a	7 a	8 c	9 b	10 a
11 b	12 b	13 a	14 b	15 a	16 a	17 b	18 b	19 b	20 c

Chapter 5 TRIGONOMETRY

Activity 9
page 85

2 **a** 43.3 m   **b** 101.0 m
3 This is the completed table:

$\theta°$	0	15	30	45	60	75	89
$\tan \theta°$	0	0.2679	0.5774	1	1.732	3.732	57.29

Tan 89° is large because the 'opposite' side becomes much larger compared to the 'adjacent' side as the angle approaches 90°.

Exercise 26
page 87

1

	a $\triangle$ABC	**b** $\triangle$XYZ	**c** $\triangle$PQR	**d** $\triangle$RST
Hypotenuse	AC	XZ	QR	RT
Opposite	AB	YZ	PR	ST
Adjacent	BC	XY	PQ	RS

2 **a** 6.66 cm   **b** 8.71 cm   **c** 8.44 cm   **d** 6.95 cm
3 **a** 4.04 cm   **b** 11.3 cm   **c** 6.54 cm   **d** 4.35 cm
4 87.5 m   5 37.3 m   6 **a** 295 mm   **b** 56.1 cm
7 14.6 m²   8 BX = 4.25 cm, CX = 2.14 cm   9 7.57 cm

Exercise 27
page 89

1 **a** 15°   **b** 30°   **c** 45°   **d** 60°   **e** 70°   **f** 75°
2 **a** 36.9°   **b** 38.0°   **c** 37.9°   **d** 67.4°
3 $\alpha = 24.3°$, $\beta = 65.7°$ 4 23.4°   5 $\alpha = 69°$, $\beta = 139°$ 6 67°
7 100.0°   8 **a** 125°   **b** 305°   9 98°

Activity 10
page 90

$\theta°$	0	15	30	45	60	90
$\sin \theta°$	0	0.259	0.500	0.707	0.866	1.000
$\cos \theta°$	1.000	0.966	0.866	0.707	0.500	0

Exercise 28
page 92

1 **a** 2.46 cm   **b** 4.59 cm   **c** 11.6 cm   **d** 345 m
2 **a** 10.6 m   **b** 16.0 m   **c** 4.13 m   **d** 5.40 m
3 1.61 m   4 67.6 m + height of end of string above ground

Chapter 5 TRIGONOMETRY

5 a 6.57 cm   b 6.60 cm   6 a 107 m   b 79.7 m
7 38.8 m   8 a 2.5 m   b 4.33 m   c 20.6 m^2 d 31.7°
9 5.88 cm   10 FT = 2.96 cm, ET = 5.56 cm, EG = 7.73 cm

Activity 11   page 93

1 Angles: 0°, 15°, 30°, 45°, 55°, 60°, 75°, 90°
2 Angles: 0°, 15°, 30°, 35°, 45°, 60°, 75°, 90°

Exercise 29   page 94

1 a 48.6°   b 26.7°   c 29.2°   d 44.4°
2 a 44.4°   b 51.1°   c 56.7°   d 41.9°
3 58.8°   4 7.18°   5 70.5°   6 23.6°
7 a 15.5 km b 014.9°   8 43.3 cm^2 9 57.3°

Exercise 30   page 96

1 a 5.14 cm   b 14.9 mm   c 45.6°   d 28.7°
2 a 61.3°   b 4.58 cm   c 65.4°   d 3.99 km
3 a $x = 5.96$ cm, $\alpha = 44.8°$ b $x = 3.07$ m, $\alpha = 39.9°$
   c $x = 10.9$ mm, $\alpha = 45.7°$ d $x = 2.46$ cm, $y = 18.1$ cm
4 15.9 m   5 17.3°   6 592 km
7 22.2 m   8 a $D = 1.41$ m   b Undesirable to have too large a 'D'.
9 a 3.64 cm   b 5.08 cm^2 10 a 20.6 m   b 19.0 m   c 20.8 m
11 7.99 km   12 3.56 m

Revision Exercise 5   page 98

1 a 5.89 cm   b 11.3 m   c $x = 63.2$ m, $\alpha = 35.1°$ d $x = 13$ cm, $\alpha = 67.4°$
2 a 5.47 cm   b 2.91 km   c 23.2°   d 63.6°
3 a $x = 5.44$ cm, $y = 8.46$ cm, $z = 6.48$ cm   b $x = 43.3$ mm
   c $x = 1.25$ m, $y = 3.11$ m, $z = 3.63$ m, $\alpha = 82°$ d $x = 9.06$ m, $y = 10.4$ m, $\alpha = 28.9°$
4 a 195 m   b 442 m
5 a 4.66 km N b 17.4 km W   6 611 m
7 Ascends in 3 minutes 52 seconds. Reaches surface with 8 seconds to spare!
8 a 29.5 cm^2 b 17.9 m^2 c 173 cm^2 d 1.83 m^2
9 a 17.2 km, 284°   b At 18 hours 11 minutes 10 seconds!
10 a 16.2 m   b 16.2 seconds   c 432 m

Chapter 5 TRIGONOMETRY

Basics Test 3 — page 100

A Calculator
1. 0.858
2. −689 000
3. 994
4. 0.0517
5. 3.02
6. 0.259

B Paper and pencil
7. 2
8. 0.38
9. 102 seconds
10. 15 300 000 cm³
11. 4 m
12. 875 m
13. 1
14. 18 km/h
15. $\frac{4a+5b}{20}$

C Mental
16. What is the cost of tickets for two adults and one child? — £28.25
17. What is the cost of tickets for three O.A.P.'s and six students? — £51
18. Mrs Lot takes her children to the cinema. She pays twenty five pounds fifty. How many children did she take? — 4
19. How many children could go for twenty six pounds? — 8
20. A party of students go to the cinema. They receive ten pounds change from one hundred and thirty pounds. How many tickets were bought? — 16
21. What is the square root of nine hundred? — 30
22. How many ninths are there in two and two thirds? — 24
23. Divide point five by point two. — 2.5
24. What is one per cent of fifty thousand? — 500
25. Subtract fifty nine pence from two pounds twenty five. — 166p

Puzzlers — page 100

1. One of the easiest methods is to place two stakes in the ground ten metres apart and find out how many times the ribbon can be wound around both stakes.

2. d is the only possibility.

3. 16 000 km each.

33

Chapter 5 TRIGONOMETRY

— COURSEWORK: Aviation flight paths page 101

MARKS (M) 4; (A) 6; (E) 3; (N) 2; (I) 1; (C) 4

It may be necessary to remind pupils about grid references, map scales and bearings before the start of this Coursework. It is a good idea to check that each pupil has copied the map correctly before starting part 2.

2 **a** Bearing of Berry Head from Land's End
    $= \tan^{-1} \frac{6}{2} = 71.57°$ to 4 SF
    $= 072°$ to nearest degree
  b Bearing from Southampton to Berry Head
    $= 180° + 72° = 252°$
  c Distance from Southampton to Land's End
    $= \frac{300}{\sin 71.57} = 316.2$ km to 4 SF

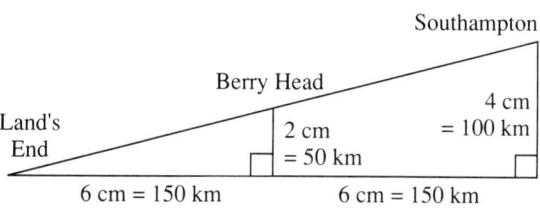

3 $\sin 1° = \frac{x}{316.2}$
   Therefore $x = 5.52$ km to 3 SF

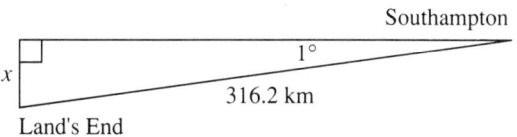

4 17 000 feet $= 5.184$ km to 4 SF
   316.2 km $= 1\,037\,000$ feet to 4 SF
   $\tan \alpha = \frac{5.184}{316.2}$
   Therefore $\alpha = 0.9°$ to 1 SF

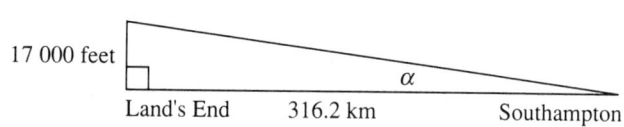

5 Distance travelled in 23.2 minutes $= \frac{450 \times 23.2}{60} = 174$ km $= 6.96$ cm on map.
  a Distance on map between Land's End and crash ≈ 9.5 cm ≈ 235 km. This is also the distance between the crash and Southampton.
  b Land's End: arrives 18:55 on a bearing of 119°. (All bearings to nearest °.)
    Berry Head: on a bearing of 162° at a speed of 87 km/h.
    Southampton: arrives 18:52.8 on a bearing of 204°. (Arrives first.)

6 By extending the air corridors the grid reference of Cork is 161405 and the grid reference of Dublin is 200440.
Bearing of Cork from Dublin
$= \beta + 180°$
$= \tan^{-1} \frac{7.8}{7} + 180°$
$= 48.09° + 180° = 228°$
Distance between Cork and Dublin
$= \frac{195}{\sin 48.09°} = 262$ km to 3 SF
Average speed of flight $= \frac{262}{0.5} = 524$ km/h

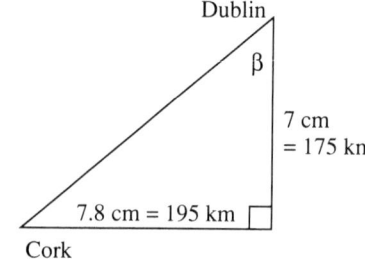

Chapter 6 PROPORTION

Exercise 31 — page 104

1 **a** 11.4 km **b** 285 km
2 **a** 9.4 hours **b** 1720.2 hours (approximately 72 days)
3 **a** 9000 **b** 9
4 **a** £7.95 **b** £55.65
5 **a** 4.5 **b** 1.5
6 **a** 135 m **b** 1182.6 km
7 **a** 2083 **b** 35
8 1500
9 £100.80
10 £3.40
11 700 m
12 £4.48
13 97.2 g
14 5000 km
15 1 minute

Activity 12 — page 105

KITCHENS UNITS CONVERTER											
MASS											
Ounces	0	4	8	12	16	20	24	28	32	36	
Grams	0	110	230	340	450	570	680	790	910	1000	
Pounds	0	$\tfrac{1}{4}$	$\tfrac{1}{2}$	$\tfrac{3}{4}$	1	$1\tfrac{1}{4}$	$1\tfrac{1}{2}$	$1\tfrac{3}{4}$	2	$2\tfrac{1}{4}$	
CAPACITY											
Litres	0	0.1	0.2	0.3	0.4	0.5	0.6	0.7	0.8	0.9	
Fluid oz	0	3.5	7.0	11	14	18	21	25	28	32	
Pints	0	$\tfrac{1}{4}$	$\tfrac{1}{2}$	$\tfrac{3}{4}$	1	$1\tfrac{1}{4}$	$1\tfrac{1}{2}$				
TEMPERATURE											
°C	120	140	160	180	200	220	240	260	280	300	
°F	250	280	320	360	390	430	460	500	540	570	
Gas		1	2	3	4	5	6	7	8	9	10	11	12

Exercise 32 — page 106

1 a
2 a
3 c
4 5000 m
5 $\tfrac{1}{2}$ pound of flour
6 Bill
7 Gill
8 Field
9 16 pint barrel
10 **a** 3 litres
11 0.5625%
12 6.77%
13 1.57%
14 1 km = 0.6214 miles
15 $\tfrac{1}{16}$ = 0.0625 inches = 1.6 mm $\tfrac{5}{64}$ = 0.078 125 inches = 2.0 mm
    $\tfrac{3}{32}$ = 0.093 75 inches = 2.4 mm $\tfrac{7}{64}$ = 0.109 375 inches = 2.8 mm
    $\tfrac{1}{8}$ = 0.125 inches = 3.2 mm $\tfrac{9}{64}$ = 0.140 625 inches = 3.6 mm
    $\tfrac{5}{32}$ = 0.156 25 inches = 4.0 mm $\tfrac{11}{64}$ = 0.171 875 inches = 4.4 mm
    $\tfrac{3}{16}$ = 0.1875 inches = 4.8 mm $\tfrac{13}{64}$ = 0.203 125 inches = 5.2 mm
    $\tfrac{7}{32}$ = 0.218 75 inches = 5.6 mm $\tfrac{15}{64}$ = 0.234 375 inches = 6.0 mm
    $\tfrac{1}{4}$ = 0.25 inches = 6.4 mm
    (Discuss why the imperial sizes are not in the the series $\tfrac{1}{16}, \tfrac{1}{15}, \tfrac{1}{14}, \tfrac{1}{13}$ etc.)
16 **a** 0.23% less to 2 SF   **b** 0.098% more to 2 SF
18 8.49×10^{56}

Chapter 6 PROPORTION

━ Activity 13   page 107

Length: 1 inch, 30 cm, 1 m, metres, miles
Volume and capacity: 1 litre, 1 gallon
Temperature: °C

Mass: 1 kilogram
Area: 1 hectare

━ Exercise 33   page 108

1   a DM 120   b DM 3.6   c DM 7.5   2   a Ptas 450   b Ptas 900   c Ptas 675
3   a $4.5   b $45   c $2.25   4   a Fr 132   b Fr 7.7   c Fr 330
5   a £2   b £4   c £0.40   6   a £5   b £9   c £14
7   a £23   b £65   c £4.25   8   a £30   b £90   c £7
9   $ 0.55 = £0.3̇6, Ptas 90 = £0.40, DM 1.3 = £0.4̇3, Fr 4.4 = £0.40. Therefore West Germany is the most expensive.

━ Activity 14   page 109

	Chicken breast	Boneless breast	Whole chicken	Chicken leg
Cost/oz	13.7p	21.6p	11.9p	13.8p
oz/£	7.29	4.63	8.41	7.24

━ Exercise 34   page 109

1   a (1977) (i) 28 g/p (ii) 20 g/p (iii) 30 g/p (iv) 28 g/p
    (1987) (v) 16 g/p (vi) 10 g/p (vii) 21 g/p (viii) 15 g/p
    Therefore best buys are (iii) (1977) and (vii) (1987).
2   55p
3   £6.69, £1.70
4   Calor Gas is 6 g/p, Camping Gas is ≈ 1.1 g/p, therefore you get approximately five times more for your money when buying Calor Gas. However, the Camping Gas cylinder is disposable.
5

Type of liquid	Cost per litre		% increase (2 SF)
	1979	1985	
Brandy	10.72	13.60	27
Ink (cartridge)	40.00	80.00	100
Petrol	0.29	0.42	45
Ink (bottle)	7.89	15.80	100
Beer	0.79	1.23	56

Chapter 6 PROPORTION

Activity 15 — page 111

1 0.22 m   **2** 4.1 m   **3** 180 m   **4** 89 m   **5** 66 m   **6** 6×10^7 m

Exercise 35 — page 111

1 53.3   **2** 18.3 days   **3** 11.9 miles   **4** 600 000 gallons   **5** 2.31 million
6 150 tonnes   **7** 0.5 g   **8** 1:1 million   **9 a** 1×10^9 **b** 0.909 g/cm³
10 3.79 seconds   **11** 30.8 kg   **12** 6.25 million   **13** £2.5 $\times 10^{11}$ **14** 456 gallons
15 1640 km   **a** 8.2 cm   **b** 164 cm   **c** 1640 cm   **d** 6560 cm
16 a 15 m   **b** 14 cm   **c** 1.2 cm²   **d** 30 m²   **17** 24 times

Activity 16 — page 113

1 12 500 men   **2** 2.5 years   **3** 100 000 ÷ t **4** 100 000 ÷ n **5** 2 years
6 (i) 4 years   (ii) 2 tunnels   (iii) 40 years   (iv) 400 000 men

Exercise 36 — page 114

1 a

Number of men	Time in days to dig		
	1 trench	2 trenches	3 trenches
1	8	16	24
2	4	8	12
4	2	4	6
3	$2\frac{2}{3}$	$5\frac{1}{3}$	8
n	$8 \div n$	$16 \div n$	$24 \div n$

b Time in days for 1 man to dig x trenches = $8x$.
c 1 day
d 2 men
e 21 trenches

2 a (i) 15 years   (ii) 60 years   (iii) 40 years   (iv) 3000 years   (v) $(120\,000 \div x)$ years
   b (i) 20 000 men   (ii) 6000 men   (iii) 120 000 men   (iv) 120 men   (v) $(120\,000 \div y)$ men
3 a 1 hour   **b** 5   **c** 500   **d** 4.5 billion
4 a 16.2 = 16 tonnes to 2 SF   **b** (i) 4 minutes   (ii) 30 seconds   (iii) 70 seconds   (iv) 8 seconds
5 a 5   **b** 1000   **c** 2.26×10^8 tonnes
6 a 80 000 tonnes   **b** 2 g   **c** (i) 219 tonnes   (ii) 440 g

Activity 17 — page 115

Distance from present time: First living cells 350 cm
First land animals 43 cm
First mammals 24 cm
Giant dinosaurs 15 cm
Man 0.44 cm

Chapter 6 PROPORTION

Exercise 37 — page 116

1. 0.743 cm^3
2. 9.42 kg
3. 11.4 tonnes
4. 288 kg
5. Aluminium weighs 106 g. Brass weighs 102 g. Therefore aluminium weighs 4 g more.
6. **a** 10.2 ohms   **b** 7.89 m
7. 12 000
8. **a** 84 J   **b** 126 J   **c** 2520 J
9. 31.5 g
10. **a** 2000   **b** 1430
11. The length is $3.\dot{3}$ times longer. $\approx$ 1 cm long.
12. **a** (i) 2.07 cm^2 (ii) 0.905 cm^2 **b** 4-day-old hamster
13. **a** 10^{27}, 27 zeros   **b** $\sqrt[3]{10^{-27}} = 10^{-9}$ **c** 10 million
    d 2×10^{23}, 2×10^{16} cm, $(2 \times 10^{16}) \div (40 \times 10^{8}) \approx 5 \times 10^{6}$ times!

Revision Exercise 6 — page 118

1. 20.9 km
2. 1.59 kg
3. 5.28 pints
4. 22.2 acres
5. £3.53
6. 7.29p
7. 355 cm^2
8. 13 stone 5.43 pounds
9. 36.9°C
10. 159%
11. Fr 36.8
12. £5.50
13. 14.8%
14. **a** 54.0p   **b** (i) 1.04 g/cm^3 (ii) 399 cm^3 (iii) No
15. 9×10^{24}
16. 18.0 m
17. 500 000
18. 2.28
19. 0.875 km
20. 4.09
21. 33 000
22. 347 000 m^3
23. **a** 25   **b** 10 g   **c** 6 million km
24. 40.2 days
25. Value of gold in 1 m^3 $\approx$ 6p and in 1 cubic yard $\approx$ 5p.

Basic Algebra Test 2 — page 120

1. $8a$
2. $12a^2$
3. $-4a$
4. $\frac{1}{3}$
5. $\frac{5x}{6}$
6. $\frac{x^2}{6}$
7. $\frac{2}{3}$
8. $\frac{-x}{6}$
9. $3a^3b$
10. $\frac{a}{3b}$
11. $1 + x$
12. $18x^2$
13. 8
14. 6
15. 16
16. 16
17. -2
18. $2\frac{1}{2}$
19. $1\frac{1}{2}$
20. $-2\frac{1}{2}$
21. $2b(1 + 2b)$
22. $ab(a - b)$
23. $x \leq -\frac{2}{3}$
24. $x < 16$
25. $\frac{17x}{20}$
26. $3abc$
27. $2b + 1$
28. $\frac{x-10}{12}$
29. -2
30. -12
31. -12
32. 9

Puzzlers — page 120

1. ①+⑦+⑩ = 18
2. 11
3. Each palindromic number is aba. There are 9 possibilities for a, that is, 1–9, and 10 possibilities for b, that is, 0–9. Therefore 9×10 gives 90 numbers.
4. 2 minutes

Chapter 6 PROPORTION

— COURSEWORK: The solar system page 121

MARKS (M) 4; (A) 6; (E) 3; (N) 2; (I) 1; (C) 4

A method to introduce this Coursework to a less able class is to work through the following:

If the Earth is represented by a basketball of diameter 23 cm, find **a** the diameter of the Sun **b** how far away the planet Pluto is, using this scale. (Stress the importance of setting out the working clearly.)

		Actual	*Model*
	Earth	12 800 km is represented by	23 cm (this is the scale)
		1 km is represented by	$\frac{23}{12\,800}$ cm ($\div$ both sides by 12 800)
a	Sun	1.39×10^6 km is represented by	$\frac{23}{12\,800} \times 1.39 \times 10^6$ cm
			= 25 m correct to 2 SF.
b	Distance of Pluto	5.95×10^9 km is represented by	$\frac{23}{12\,800} \times 5.59 \times 10^9$ cm
			= 100 km correct to 1 SF

1 a Diameter of planet model (cm) = $\left[\dfrac{\text{ht. of room (cm)}}{1.39 \times 10^6}\right] \times$ actual diameter of planet (km)

[ ] is the multiplying factor which should be put into the Memory.

Scale $n = \dfrac{1.39 \times 10^{11}}{\text{ht. of room (cm)}}$

b Diameters in mm to 2 SF: Mercury 6.8, Venus 17, Earth 18, Mars 9.5, Saturn 170, Uranus 71, Neptune 67, Pluto 4.
(i) Diameter of Sun 1900 mm
(ii) Diameter of largest star 52 000 mm = 52 m
Diameter of model (mm) = $\dfrac{200}{1.43 \times 10^5} \times$ actual diameter in km

2 a Distance in cm to 2 SF: Mercury 4.9, Venus 9.1, Earth 13, Mars 19, Jupiter 65, Saturn 120, Uranus 240, Neptune 380.
b Nearest star 33.4 km
c (i) Divide by 100   (ii) Divide by 25   (iii) Multiply by 20

3 Time for light to reach Earth to 2 SF: Mercury 310 seconds, Venus 140 seconds, Mars 260 seconds, Jupiter 35 minutes, Saturn 71 minutes, Uranus 150 minutes, Neptune 4.0 hours, Pluto 5.4 hours, nearest star 4.2 years.
Last answer shows that the nearest star is 4.2 light years away.

4 Time for space craft to reach the planets to 2 SF: Mercury 96 days, Venus 44 days, Mars 81 days, Jupiter 1.8 years, Saturn 3.7 years, Uranus 7.8 years, Neptune 12 years, Pluto 17 years. Nearest star 110 000 years.

Chapter 7 ALGEBRA II

Activity 18 — page 122

Input (I)	(II)	(III)	Output (IV)
2	4	12	13
5	25	75	76
7	49	147	148
x	x^2	$3x^2$	$3x^2 + 1$
7	49	147	148
1	1	3	4
3	9	27	28
$\sqrt{y}$	y	$3y$	$3y + 1$

Input (I)	(II)	(III)	Output (IV)
6	36	108	109
4	16	48	49
9	81	243	244
$\sqrt{[(p-1)/3]}$	$(p-1)/3$	$p-1$	p
11	121	363	364
3	9	27	28
5	25	75	76
$\sqrt{(q/3)}$	$q/3$	q	$q+1$

Activity 19 — page 123

This activity has proved very successful and is well worth spending 10–15 minutes on.

Exercise 38 — page 124

1 2	**2** 3	**3** 9	**4** 2
5 9	**6** 38	**7** $2\frac{1}{2}$	**8** 30
9 −2	**10** $2\frac{1}{2}$	**11** 16	**12** 24
13 29	**14** 7	**15** ±5	**16** ±3
17 ±7	**18** ±10	**19** ±9	**20** ±5
21 ±9	**22** ±13	**23** ±0.8	**24** ±1.2
25 ±5	**26** ±14	**27** ±10	**28** ±14
29 ±1.2	**30** ±0.9	**31** 12	**32** 576
33 −1	**34** 98	**35** 36	**36** 194
37 196	**38** 1		
39 10	**40** 256	**41** 10	**42** 10
43 5	**44** 10	**45** 2.5, 5.5	**46** ±1.5
47 2.40	**48** 243	**49** 1, 97	**50** 3.54, 10.46 (2 DP)

Activity 20 — page 125

$6\,\text{m}^2 < x < 7\,\text{m}^2$
b (i) 8.5 cm (ii) 9.2 cm (iii) 10.7 cm (iv) 11.3 cm

Exercise 39 — page 126

1 **a** 5.5 cm   **b** 3.6 m   **c** 18.5 mm   **d** 0.35 km
2 **a** ±4.36   **b** ±1.53   **c** ±1.58   **d** ±1.66

3   a 4.5 cm, 18 cm   b 5.25 cm, 21 m
4   2.25 cm   5 a 1.5 m   b 36 m^2
6   2.25 m × 0.5 m   7 1.8 m × 0.9 m × 0.4 m

___ Activity 21   page 128

G   Number of GCSEs $G \geq 8$
A: Number of A levels $A \geq 3$
a: Number of years old $a > 18$
S: Shorthand in wpm $S \geq 120$
T: Typing in wpm $T \geq 60$
H: Hours of work $H \geq 35$
D: Dollars per annum $15\,000 \leq D \leq 18\,000$

___ Exercise 40   page 128

1   a W Weight of vehicle, in tons $W < 30$ tons
    b N Number of half-price CDs $N > 1000$
    c M Percentage mark $62 \leq M \leq 74$
    d P Number of people in the chalets $2 \leq P \leq 8$
2   $6 \leq L \leq 8$ 3 $1.5 \leq h \leq 2$
4   $62.5 \leq t \leq 64$ 5 $90 \leq d \leq 135$
6   $4N + 50 \leq 350$, $N_{max} = 75$ 7 $5N + 80 < 830$, $N_{max} = 149$
8   $0.25m + 125 < 312.50$, $m_{max} = 750$ (approximately!)

___ Activity 22   page 129

It could be worth discussing other ways in which π can be calculated ...

___ Activity 23   page 130

1   The memory function on the calculator should be used. Distances to 3 SF are 15.4 m, 30.8 m, 46.2 m, 61.6 m, 77.0 m, 92.4 m.
    Circumference of wheel = 153.9 cm to 4 SF
    The graph of number of revolutions against distance is a straight line, with a gradient of the wheel circumference.
2   The trundle wheel may not have been rolled in a straight line; there may be cumulative errors from measurements 'by eye'.

Chapter 7 ALGEBRA II

—— Exercise 41 — page 131

1 **a** 18.8 cm   **b** 50.3 m   **c** 105 cm   **d** 214 m   **e** 11.9 mm   **f** 1340 cm
2 **a** 9.42 cm   **b** 22.0 m   **c** 62.2 m   **d** 176 m   **e** 56.5 mm   **f** 440 cm
3 **a** 19.6 cm   **b** 7.16 m   **c** 15.6 cm   **d** 2.55 mm   **e** 1.97 m   **f** 66.8 mm
4 The circle, with circumference $\approx$ 40.02 cm
5 44.6 cm   6 **a** 330 cm **b** 90 000
7 **a** 188 cm   **b** 53 100   **c** 53 100   **d** 14.7
8 64 500 mph   9 15 400 mph
10 **a** (i) 1040 km/h (ii) 1670 km/h   **b** (i) 780 km (ii) 1250 km
11 **a** 318   **b** 2.65   **c** 80   12 4.66 m
13 15.9 miles   14 556 m
15 **a** 15.4 cm   **b** 17.9 cm   16 220 m

—— Activity 24 — page 133

It should be mentioned that the longer side of the rectangle approaches a straight line as the number of sectors increases.

—— Exercise 42 — page 135

1 **a** 50.3 cm^2 **b** 150 cm^2 **c** 452 mm^2 **d** 163 m^2 **e** 2830 m^2 **f** 7030 mm^2
2 **a** 1.64 cm   **b** 0.977 cm   **c** 3.83 mm   **d** 1.60 m   **e** 3.83 m   **f** 3.14 km
3 **a** 2.52 cm   **b** 3.19 cm   **c** 2.74 mm   **d** 3.39 m   **e** 4.05 m   **f** 12.9 km
4 1.77 ha
5 Area of circle = 106 cm^2 (3 SF)
6 **a** 19.2 cm^2 **b** 32.3 cm^2 **c** 66.3 cm^2
7 10.5 cm^2 for each figure
8 5.30 cm^2
9 **a** 5.05 cm   **b** 10.7 cm   **c** 120 m   **d** 4.37 cm
10 **a** 6.87 cm^2 **b** 1.93 cm^2 **c** 6.18 cm^2 **d** 5.50 cm^2 **e** 925 mm^2
11 810 cm^2
12 10 in a row $\approx$ 25.9 cm, therefore $r \approx$ 1.295 cm, therefore A = 5.27 cm^2 (3 SF).
13 **a** 5.14 cm^2 **b** 1.28 cm^2
14 **a** (i) 23.3 m (ii) 46.6 m   **b** (i) 1710 m^2 (ii) 6830 m^2 **c** $A = \pi h^2 \tan^2(\frac{\theta}{2})$
    A graph of A against h could be a useful investigation.
15 8.37 cm
16 Area = $\frac{2r}{2\pi r} \times \pi r^2 = r^2$

Chapter 7 ALGEBRA II

— Activity 25   page 137

2 The largest square has the same area as the total of the two smaller squares.
3 Areas in cm^2: '1' = x^2, '2' = $\frac{x^2}{4}$ [= 6], '3' = $\frac{3x^2}{4}$ '4' = x^2, '5' = $\frac{7x^2}{4}$
   The areas of the two largest squares are $5x^2$ and $4x^2$.

— Exercise 43   page 138

1 **a** 6.40 cm   **b** 2.30 cm   **c** 9.85 cm   **d** 80.8 mm   **e** 8.37 cm   **f** 8.26 m
2 19.6 m
3 129 cm
4

	AD	DB	AB	BC	Area (cm^2)
a	3	4	5	8	12
b	6	8	10	16	48
c	5.66	7	9	14	39.6
d	5	4.9	7.00	9.8	24.5
e	2.78	7.5	8	15	20.9
f	4.5	10	11.0	20	45
g	8	2.25	8.31	4.5	18

5 **a** 2.5 m   **b** 6.5 m^2
6 50 cm^2
7 449 m
8 13 units
9 No
10 8.94 miles
11 24 m
12 Obtuse
13 3.84 cm^2
14 4 m
15 11.2 cm
16 **a** $A = \frac{C^2}{4\pi}$ **b** 3.71 cm
17 Let angle ACX = $a°$, angle CBY = $b°$ and AX = x
    AB = BC (first fold)
    AC = BC (second fold)
    Therefore triangle ABC is equilateral.
    Therefore $a° = b° = 30°$
    Therefore AC = BC = AB = $2x$
    CX = $x\sqrt{3}$, OC = $\frac{2x}{\sqrt{3}}$, OX = $\frac{x}{\sqrt{3}}$
    Therefore $\frac{CO}{2}$ = OX
    This method of folding can be used to make angles of 30° and 60°.
18 Answers to 3 SF: AD = 14.4 cm, BD = 4.17 cm, BC = 8.34 cm *or* AD = 4.17 cm, BD = 14.4 cm, BC = 28.8 cm

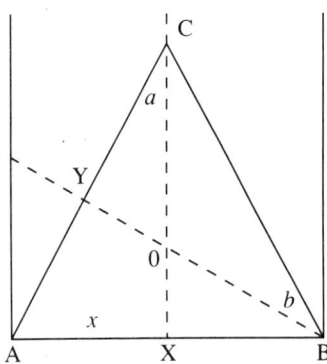

Chapter 7 ALGEBRA II

── Exercise 44   page 142

1   a 3770 cm^3 b $23\,600$ cm^3 c 1180 cm^3 d $46\,200$ cm^3
2   a 75.4 cm^2 b 226 cm^2 c 149 cm^2 d 1260 cm^2
3   a 44.4 cm   b 47.9 cm   c 44.4 cm   d 52.1 cm (AB, here, is the diagonal of the rectangle.)
4

	Height (cm)	Volume (cm^3)	Curved surface area (cm^2)	AB (cm)
a	0.140	11	4.40	31.4
b	0.280	22	8.80	31.4
c	1.43	112	45	31.4
d	2.86	225	90	31.5
e	157	12 300	4930	160
f	318	25 000	10 000	320

5   $r = 3.750$ cm to 4 SF. Dimensions: 30.0 cm $\times$ 22.5 cm
6   (It is not recommended that any answers are verified by practical experiment!)
7   Density $= 0.985$ g/cm^3

── Exercise 45   page 143

1   a 50.3 b 804 c 3220 2   a 2.50 b 9.09 c 7.61
3   a 33.5 b 268 c 65.4 4   a 10.0 b 36 c 26.3
5   a 50.1 b 143 c 490 6   a 2.11 b 2.46 c 3.17
7   a (i) 15.7 m/s   (ii) 22.1 m/s   (iii) 99.0 m/s   b 4910 m
8   a 75.0 m/s   b 61.0 m/s   c 71.6 m/s
9   a $A = 2(c + b - a)$ b (i) 4 cm^2 (ii) 8 cm^2 (iii) 20 cm^2
10   a (i) 16 (ii) 18 (iii) $2n + 6$ b 47

── Exercise 46   page 145

1   $x = \frac{y}{4}$ 2 $x = \frac{y}{p}$ 3 $x = h - a$ 4 $x = \frac{1}{2}(g + h)$
5   $x = \frac{1}{2}(t - r)$ 6 $x = \frac{1}{3}(2 - a)$ 7 $x = \frac{w-z}{y}$ 8 $x = \frac{p-r}{s}$
9   $x = \frac{ut-v}{t}$ 10 $x = \frac{gh-c}{d}$ 11 $x = \frac{3}{y}$ 12 $x = \frac{ab}{y}$
13   $x = \frac{t}{s-v}$ 14 $x = \frac{rt}{k+1}$ 15 $x = \frac{b}{a-y}$ 16 $x = \frac{gh}{1-z}$
17   $x = \frac{f}{a} - g$ 18 $x = \frac{k}{a} + g$ 19 $x = \frac{a-wb}{w}$ 20 $x = \frac{fb-a}{f}$
21   $x = \frac{a^2-v^2}{2a}$ 22 $x = \frac{a-b^2}{c}$ 23 $x = \frac{dc-r^2}{h}$ 24 $x = \frac{3\pi - f}{t\pi}$
25   $x = \pm\sqrt{\frac{A}{\pi}}$ 26 $x = \frac{A}{\pi(a+h)}$ 27 $x = \frac{d}{mn-b}$ 28 $x = \frac{A-Ba}{B}$
29   $x = \frac{b}{(a+b)c}$ 30 $x = \frac{a^2}{b-c}$ 31 $x = \frac{g^2}{f+h}$ 32 $x = \frac{d}{2c^2-b}$
33   $x = \frac{2z}{3y} + 1$ 34 $x = 1 - \frac{3z}{2y}$ 35 $x = y^2$ 36 $x = 2y^2$

37 $a = \frac{2(y-ut)}{t^2}$ **a** 12   **b** 8   **c** 6.25

38 $l = \frac{A}{\pi r} - r = \frac{A - \pi r^2}{\pi r}$ **a** 1.18   **b** 7.89   **c** 18.9

39 $r = \sqrt[3]{\frac{3V}{4\pi}}$ **a** 1.34   **b** 3.10   **c** 5.79

── Revision Exercise 7   page 146

1   **a** 8   **b** −15   **c** −2   **d** 16
2   **a** ±6   **b** ±4   **c** ±18   **d** ±26
3   **a** 64   **b** 144   **c** 97   **d** 180.5
4   **a** 9.5   **b** 2.7   **c** 1.5, −2.5   **d** 6.3, −4.3
5   **a** 47.1 m $\leq C \leq$ 69.1 m, therefore **c** (i) C_{max} = 69.1 m
     b 177 m² $\leq A \leq$ 380 m², therefore **c** (ii) A_{min} = 177 m²
6   **a** 21 + 5L + 6T $\leq$ 75 or 5L + 6T $\leq$ 54   **b** 10
7   **a** (i) 59 °F (ii) 68 °F (iii) 5 °F
     b $C = \frac{5(F-32)}{9}$ (i) 30 °C (ii) 20 °C (iii) −40 °C
     c −40 °F or −40 °C
8 $A = \frac{1}{2}(a+c)b$ **a** 270 cm²   **b** $c = \frac{2A}{b} - a$ (i) 15 m (ii) 24.95 mm
9   **a** (i) 44.0 cm (ii) 154 cm²   **b** (i) 12.6 m (ii) 12.6 m²
     c (i) 134 mm (ii) 942 mm²   **d** (i) 58.8 cm (ii) 225 cm²
10   **a** 8.06 cm   **b** 10.2 m   **c** 5.66 mm   **d** 8.72 cm
11   13.4 cm   **12** 0.0251 litres/sec   **13** 0.230 m   **14** 100π cm²   **15** 42857

── Aural Test 2   page 148

1   A packet of flour weighs four point four pounds. Approximately how many kilograms is this?   2
2   What is the density of a stone of mass 234 g and a volume of 65 cm³?   3.6 g/cm³
3   Mr Rushdie buys a number of nineteen pence stamps. If the total cost was three pounds eighty, how many stamps did he buy?   20
4   What is five per cent of four hundred and eighty?   24
5   Change three thousand eight hundred cubic centimetres to litres.   3.8 litres
6   Six note books cost seven pounds eighty. How much do five cost?   £6.50
7   What is the sine ratio of ninety degrees?   1
8   Miss Todd cycles twelve miles at an average speed of eighteen miles per hour. How many minutes did she take?   40
9   A race lasted thirty nine minutes and finished at thirteen fifteen. What time did it start?   12:36

(Continued)

Chapter 7 ALGEBRA II

10 When *b* equals minus three what is the value of *b* cubed?   −27
11 Name the shape OFED.   Rhombus
12 What is the size of the angle ABC?   120°
13 How many times will five point two divide into
    twenty four point nine six?   4.8
14 What is the total cost of five two hour lessons
    and three one hour lessons?   £170
15 Which town is nearest to London?   Oxford
16 Which two towns are approximately three hundred
    and twenty kilometres apart?   Manchester and London
17 A girl drives from London to Manchester via Oxford.
    How far does she drive?   209 miles
18 The horizontal distance between A and B is one
    hundred and fifty metres. Find the gradient of slope AB.   1/30
19 The mean gradient between A and C is 1:20. What is
    the horizontal distance between A and C?   200 m
20 Which of the masses shown is about the mass of an adult?   a: 75 kg

▬ Puzzlers   page 148

1 There are about 900 000, six-digit numbers and about 90 000 five-digit numbers. This is about 99% of all the numbers.
   Let t = time to say a five-digit number and n = the number of times longer it takes to say a six-digit number.
   Approximate time = $\frac{90\,000t}{3600 \times 24} + \frac{900\,000tn}{3600 \times 24} \approx 104t(10n + 1)$ days

2 | A | B | C | D | | A | B | C | D | | A | B | C | D |
   |---|---|---|---|---|---|---|---|---|---|---|---|---|---|
   | B | A | D | C | | C | A | D | B | | D | A | B | C |
   | B | D | A | C | | C | D | A | B | | D | C | A | B |
   | B | C | D | A | | C | D | B | A | | D | C | B | A |

3 EATT = 207
   TEET = 222
   Therefore A = E − 15
   AAPT = 183
   Therefore PEAT = 183 + 15 = 198

4 There are 45 dots. Therefore the
   triangle must pass through 7 dots.
   This is one solution:

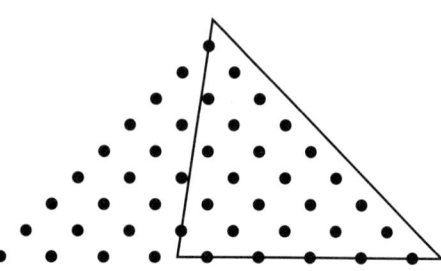

Chapter 7 ALGEBRA II

— COURSEWORK: The Active Maths puzzle   page 149

MARKS (M) 3; (A) 6; (E) 3; (N) 3; (I) 1; (C) 4

Pupils who have worked from Books 1 and 2 may remember this fascinating puzzle. Stress the importance of constructing the 90° angle accurately.

1 Diagram showing all the lines which are equal in length to the diagonal of piece IV.

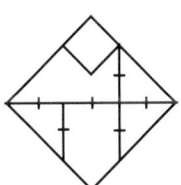

2 a Diagram showing how a right angle is constructed.

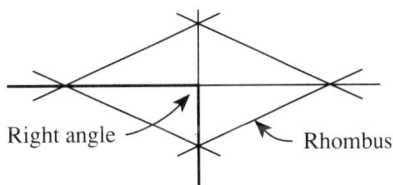

3 a BA is the width of a grid square.
   b Area of triangle ABC = 8 cm². $AD^2 + BD^2 = 16$. But AD = BD.
      Therefore $2AD^2 = 16$, $AD^2 = 8$ and AD = 2.828 cm to 4 SF
      Therefore area of triangle ABD = $(2.828)^2 \div 2 = 4$ cm²

4

Piece number	Area (cm²)	Perimeter (cm) to 3 SF
I	8	13.7
IV	8	11.3
V	20	17.7
VI	20	23.3

5 a Side length = hypotenuse of piece I
                  + side length of piece IV
      = (1.414 × 4) + (0.7071 × 4)
      = 8.49 cm² to 3 SF
   b Side length = the square root of the total area of the 6 pieces.
      = $\sqrt{72}$ = 8.49 cm² to 3 SF

6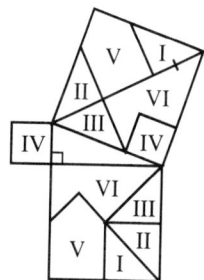

7 Area of I, II, III, IV = $0.5x^2$
   Area of V and VI = $1.25x^2$
   $(4 \times 0.5x^2) + (2 \times 1.25x^2)$
   $= (0.5x^2) + (2 \times 1.25x^2) + (3 \times 0.5x^2)$
   Therefore $2x^2 + 2.5x^2 = 0.5x^2 + 2.5x^2 + 1.5x^2$
   Therefore $4.5x^2 = 4.5x^2$, which demonstrates Pythagoras' theorem algebraically.

Chapter 7 ALGEBRA II

── FACT FINDERS: The Channel Tunnel   page 150

1. $1994 - 1802 = 192$ years

2. Percentage of tunnel under channel $= \frac{23.6}{30.7} \times 100 = 76.9\%$

3. Volume of air $= 2(\pi 3.8^2 \times 30.7 \times 1600) + \pi 2.4^2 \times 30.7 \times 1600$
   $= 4\,457\,000 + 888\,900$ to 4 SF $= 5.37 \times 10^6$ m^3

4. Cost $= (1.15 \times 2 \times 30.7 \times 1600 \times 2 \times \pi \times 3.8) + (30.7 \times 1600 \times 2 \times \pi \times 2.4 \times 1.15)$
   $= £2\,697\,000 + £851\,800$ to 4 SF $= £3.55 \times 10^6$

5. Time $= \left(\frac{2}{3} \times \frac{30.7 \times 1600}{300}\right) + \left(\frac{1}{3} \times \frac{30.7 \times 1600}{300}\right) = 164$ weeks

6. Litres/day $= 9 \times 4.5 \times 60^2 \times 24 = 3.5 \times 10^6$
   Volume of pool $= 7.5 \times 10^5$ litres
   Therefore approximately five times more than the pool.

7. Cost/second $= \frac{6 \times 10^9}{7 \times 365.25 \times 24 \times 60 \times 60} = £27.16$

8. Minimum time saved $= 100 - \left(\frac{50}{90} \times 100\right) = 44.4\%$
   Maximum time saved $= 100 - \left(\frac{45}{100} \times 100\right) = 55\%$

9. Approximate waiting time $= 3 - \frac{75}{150} - 0.75 - \frac{150}{150} = 0.75$ hours $= 45$ minutes

10. From the photograph, the height of the man on the drill face is approximately 1.4 cm, and the diameter of the drill head is about 7.4 cm. Assuming that the man is 6 feet tall (2×0.9144 m), the approximate diameter of the drill head is: $\frac{2 \times 0.9144}{1.4} \times 7.4 \approx 9.7$ m

── MULTIPLE CHOICE TEST 2A   page 246

For Chapters 5 to 7.

1 a	2 b	3 c	4 a	5 d	6 b	7 c	8 a	9 d	10 a
11 d	12 b	13 c	14 b	15 c	16 d	17 d	18 a	19 c	20 a

── MULTIPLE CHOICE TEST 2B   page 248

For Chapters 5 to 7.

1 b	2 d	3 c	4 c	5 c	6 d	7 c	8 b	9 c	10 c
11 a	12 a	13 c	14 a	15 a	16 b	17 d	18 d	19 a	20 b

Chapter 8 GRAPHS II

Activity 27 — page 153

1

x	-2	0	2
y	-8	0	8

3 Gradient = 4: if $y = 4x$ the gradient is 4. Similarly if $y = mx$, the gradient is m.

Activity 28 — page 153

1

	Equation	x	-2	0	2
a	$y = x$	y	-2	0	2
b	$y = 2x$	y	-4	0	4
c	$y = 3x$	y	-6	0	6
d	$y = 5x$	y	-10	0	10
e	$y = -2x$	y	4	0	-4
f	$y = -4x$	y	8	0	-8
g	$y = \frac{x}{2}$	y	-1	0	1
h	$y = -\frac{x}{2}$	y	1	0	-1

3

Equation	Gradient	Equation	Gradient
$y = x$	1	$y = 2x$	2
$y = 3x$	3	$y = 5x$	5
$y = -2x$	-2	$y = -4x$	-4
$y = \frac{x}{2}$	$\frac{1}{2}$	$y = -\frac{x}{2}$	$-\frac{1}{2}$

Exercise 47 — page 154

1 b (i) 25 m/s (ii) 1.8 seconds   **c** $v = 10t$

2 a

n (£)	0	10	20	30
d (DM)	0	30	60	90

c (i) DM 75 (ii) £16.67   **d** $d = 3n$

3 a

Angle $\theta°$	0	90	180	270	360
Area A (cm^2)	0	7.07	14.1	21.2	28.3

c (i) 9.42 cm² (ii) 23.6 cm²   **d** (i) 127° (ii) 318°   **e** $A = \frac{\pi\theta}{40}$

Chapter 8 GRAPHS II

— Activity 29 — page 155

	Equation	x	-2	0	2	Gradient	Intercept with y axis
(i)	$y = x - 1$	y	-3	-1	1	1	-1
(ii)	$y = -x + 1$	y	3	1	-1	-1	1
(iii)	$y = 2x - 1$	y	-5	-1	3	2	-1
(iv)	$y = -2x + 1$	y	5	1	-3	-2	1
(v)	$y = 3x - 1$	y	-7	-1	5	3	-1
(vi)	$y = -3x + 1$	y	7	1	-5	-3	1
	$y = ax + b$					a	b

— Exercise 48 — page 155

1 **a** 1, (0, 2)   **b** 2, (0, 3)   **c** 3, (0, 1)
    d 4, (0, −2)   **e** 3, (0, $\frac{3}{2}$)   **f** −3, (0, −1)

2 **a**

A (m^2)	2	4	6	8	10
C (£)	19	31	43	55	67

   c (i) £37 (ii) 7 m^2 **d** 'Call out' or estimate charge.

3 **a**

E (litres)	1.0	1.2	1.6	1.8	**3.0**
D (km)	11.5	**10.8**	9.4	**8.7**	4.5

   c (i) 9.75 km (ii) 2 litres

4 **a**

t (hours)	0	1	2	4
C (£)	3	19	35	67

   c

t (hours)	0	1	2	4
C (£)	9	13	17	25

   e (i) Mr Smart £16/hr (ii) $\frac{1}{2}$ hour, £11 (iii) Mrs Bright by £30   **f** $C = 14t + 3$

5 **a**

		A	1	10	20
Carpet P	C		41	176	326
Carpet Q	C		5	176	366

   c (i) 10 m^2 (ii) Carpet P: £251, Carpet Q: £271, therefore Carpet P is £20 more.
       (iii) Carpet P: 14.9 m^2, Carpet Q: 13.9 m^2, therefore Carpet P ≈ 1 m^2 more.

Chapter 8 GRAPHS II

— Activity 30 *page 157*

Equation	x	−2	−1	0	1	2
$y = x^2$	y	4	1	0	1	4
$y = 2x^2$	y	8	2	0	2	8
$y = -x^2$	y	−4	−1	0	−1	−4
$y = -2x^2$	y	−8	−2	0	−2	−8

— Exercise 49 *page 158*

1 a

x	−4	−2	−1	0	1	2	4
y	−8	−2	−0.5	0	−0.5	−2	−8

c 28.3 m
d Satellite dish, lights from a lamp-shade, electric-bar heater, etc.

2 a

v (m/s)	0	10	20	30	40
d (m)	**0**	**8**	**32**	**72**	**128**

c (i) 50 m (ii) 17.7 m/s   **d** Reaction time

3 a

t (s)	0	1	2	3
s (m)	0	**4.90**	**19.6**	**44.1**

c (i) 30.6 m (ii) 2.26 s   **d** 57.6 m

4 a $v = 2x^2$
b

x (m)	0	0.4	0.8	1.2	1.6
v (m³)	0	**0.32**	**1.28**	**2.88**	**5.12**

d (i) 1.41 m (ii) 0.72 m³   **e** 1.22 m < x ⩽ 1.50 m

5 a $k = 2.25$
b

t (s)	2	4	6	8	10
p	9	**36**	**81**	**144**	**225**

d (i) 56 (ii) 7 weeks
(*Note*: the first impression gives 10 in the table instead of 9, to be corrected on next printing.)

Chapter 8 GRAPHS II

Activity 32 — page 160

(As x approaches 0, y approaches infinity.)

Equation	x	-3	-2	-1	0	1	2	3
$y = \frac{3}{x}$	y	-1	-1.5	-3	∞	3	1.5	1
$y = -\frac{3}{x}$	y	1	1.5	3	∞	-3	-1.5	-1

Exercise 50 — page 160

1 a

t (months)	0	1	2	3	4	5	6
Y	$\varnothing$	2000	1000	666.7	500	400	333.3

c (i) 4 months (ii) $2\frac{2}{3}$ months

2 a

t (hours)	1	5	10	15	20
V (m³)	1000	200	100	66.7	50

c (i) 4 hours (ii) 62.5 m³

3 a

m (minutes)	5	6	7	8	9	10
T (°C)	80	66.7	57.1	50	44.4	40

c (i) 53.3 °C (ii) 6 minutes 40 seconds
d 5 minutes 20 seconds $\leq t \leq$ 8 minutes

4 a

t (days)	30	31	32	33	34	35
W (kg)	80	77.4	75	72.7	70.6	68.6

c 32.4 days
d When t is very small, W is very large. When t is very large, W is very small.

5 $y = -4$
x and y axes are asymptotes to $y = -\frac{10}{x}$.

Revision Exercise 8 — page 162

1 a $y = x$, $(x \geq 0)$ **b** $y = 2x + 1$, $(x \geq 0)$ **c** $y = -x + 3$, $(x \geq 0)$ **d** $y = 5$
e $y = 2x^2$, $(x \geq 0)$ **f** $y = \frac{3}{x}$, $(x > 0)$

3 a (i) 3 (ii) (0, 1) (iii) $(-\frac{1}{3}, 0)$ **b** (i) -3 (ii) $(0, -1)$ (iii) $(-\frac{1}{3}, 0)$
  c (i) $2\frac{1}{2}$ (ii) (0, 3) (iii) $(-1\frac{1}{5}, 0)$ **d** (i) -3 (ii) (0, 4) (iii) $(1\frac{1}{3}, 0)$

Chapter 8 GRAPHS II

4 a

M (m²)	0	5	10	15	20	25
Y (yd²)	0	**4.18**	**8.36**	**12.5**	**16.7**	20.9

c 'Earth' tiles by £182.

5 a

x (years)	0	30	60	90	120
h (m)	1.89	**2.04**	**2.19**	**2.34**	**2.49**

c (i) 1950: 2.14 m; 2000: 2.39 m (ii) 2002 (assuming pattern continues!)
d Athletes will never jump 10 m, say, therefore a limit exists.

6 a

t (s)	1	2	5	10	15	20
v (m/s)	10	**5**	**2**	1	**0.67**	0.5

c $v = 0.8\dot{3}$ m/s at $t = 12$, therefore a smooth landing.

7 a

L (cm)	0	5	10	15	20
A (cm²)	0	**5.37**	**21.5**	**48.3**	**85.8**

c (i) 30.9 cm² (ii) 15.3 cm
d A is independent of n, that is, the shaded area of a square containing n circles arranged as shown is constant.

Basics Test 4   page 164

A Calculator
  1 0.143
  3 ±2.52
  5 0.002 69

  2 7.56
  4 1.37
  6 0.0918

B Paper and pencil
  7 8
  9 $1\frac{3}{5}$
 11 20%
 13 1.2
 15 600 m

  8 $1\frac{1}{12}$
 10 £15.60
 12 11.145 kg
 14 1.25

Chapter 8 GRAPHS II

C Mental

16 How far is it between junction twenty and junction seventeen?   40 miles
17 Approximately, how many kilometres is it between junctions seventeen and nineteen?   40
18 Joan's car averages 39 miles per gallon. What fraction of a gallon does she use between junctions seventeen and eighteen? $\frac{1}{3}$
19 A car takes fifty three minutes to go from junction sixteen to junction twenty. What was its average speed?   60 mph
20 Mr Mansell averages eighty miles per hour. How long does he take between junctions seventeen and twenty?   30 minutes

21 Subtract eighteen from ninety four.   76
22 Multiply nought point three by nought point eight.   0.24
23 What is an eighth of one half? $\frac{1}{16}$
24 Divide three point four by one hundred.   0.034
25 What is the cube root of two hundred and sixteen?   6

Puzzlers   page 164

1 Let the distance travelled = a miles and let the diameter of wheel = d inches.

$$\text{Number of revolutions} = \frac{36 \times 1760 \times a}{\pi d}.$$

2 $60°$ since AC = AB = BC.

3 ... 24, 23 ... (lowest number with three letters, four letters ...)

4 There are two solutions:

$$4 \, | \, \underline{7852} \qquad 4 \, | \, \underline{6952}$$
$$ 1963 \qquad 1738$$

Chapter 8 GRAPHS II

— COURSEWORK: Bicycle gears   page 165

MARKS (M) 3; (A) 5; (E) 4; (N) 3; (I) 2; (C) 3

The actual 'gear size' of a bicycle is the ratio of the number of teeth on the pedal wheel to the number of teeth on the sprocket wheel, multiplied by the diameter of the road wheel. To most pupils this is a rather meaningless concept. In the Coursework, as a measure of gear size, we have used the distance the bicycle can travel with one complete revolution of the pedal wheel.

1 a There are twice as many teeth on the pedal wheel.
   b The sprocket wheel is fixed to the rear wheel.
   c The circumference of the rear wheel is πd.

Number of teeth in		Number of rotations of rear wheel	Distance in inches moved by bicycle
Pedal wheel	Sprocket wheel		
30	15	2	$2\pi d$
20	10	2	$2\pi d$
10	10	1	πd
60	15	4	$4\pi d$
N	n	$N \div n$	$(N \div n)\pi d$

2 A brief description of how the measurement was made of the distance moved by the bicycle with one complete revolution, is expected to include comments on how this can be done with as much accuracy as possible. All results should be tabulated.

3 The five lines should pass through the following speeds when $R = 120$ rpm: 35.7 mph, 29.4 mph, 25.0 mph, 20.8 mph, 17.8 mph.
   a Speed = $36 - 17.5 = 18.5$ mph   **b** Third gear
   c Possible pedalling speeds = 50 rpm, 61 rpm, 72 rpm, 87 rpm, 101 rpm (± 1).

4 There are three variables in the formula $100 = 0.08 \times \frac{N}{n} \times R$ and each should be considered in turn. For practical reasons R is not likely to be more than 150 rpm and n cannot be less than about 7, to give a sprocket of 2.5 cm in diameter.
The diagram shows an arrangement which would produce the same effect as a pedal wheel with 200 teeth.

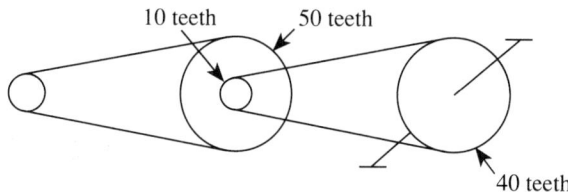

If R is the rate of pedalling per minute and the diameter of the rear wheel is 26 inches, the distance moved per hour is:

$R \times \frac{N}{n} \times \frac{\pi \times 26 \times 60}{36 \times 1760}$ miles $\approx 0.08 \times \frac{N}{n} \times R$ miles

Chapter 9 ARITHMETIC II

Exercise 51 — page 166

1 a '3.4 and 3.6'   b '12.1 and 13.1'   c '5.59 and 5.61'   d '10.15 and 10.25'
2 a 2.6 ± 0.1 b 12.25 ± 0.05 c 21.35 ± 0.05 d 8.2 ± 0.05
3 a Maximum length = 18.3 cm, minimum length = 17.9 cm
   b Minimum difference = 6.7 cm
4 w_{max} 4.98 cm, $w_{min} = 4.01\dot{6}$ cm
5 $y_{max} = 2.375$ cm, $y_{min} = 2$ cm, tolerance = 0.375 cm
6 $h_{max} = 5.685°$, $h_{min} = 4.561°$, tolerance = 1.124°
7 $p_{max} = 1.818$ kg, $p_{min} = 1.402$ kg, tolerance = 0.416 kg
8 $x_{max} = 1080$ m, $x_{min} = 779$ m, tolerance = 301 m
   Small angle errors result in large errors over a 'long' distance.

Exercise 52 — page 168

1 a 1.15   b 1.34   c 1.65   d 1.05
   e 2.10   f 2.76   g 3.00   h 1.001
2 a 0.9   b 0.85   c 0.55   d 0.95
   e 0.28   f 0.05   g 0.975   h 0.999
3

Old price (£)	% increase	New price (£)	Old price (£)	% decrease	New price (£)
1250	20	**1500**	1600	5	**1520**
750	58	**1185**	18	24	**13.68**
25	5	**26.25**	940	62	**357.20**
180	115	**387**	**95**	18	77.90
45	16	52.20	**28**	65	9.80
32	**35**	43.20	35	**14**	30.10

4 Rajind's by £104.80.
5 a £6800   b £5780   c £4913   6 a £5750   b £6612.50   c £7604.38
7 a 16%   b 19%   8 £44 880
9 12.5%   10 a £8.19   b £2.40
11 200   12 Between six and seven years
13 a £9408.54   b £4426.03   c £2082.12   d £979.49
14 £15 470.74   15 £4 392 862.05

Exercise 53 — page 171

1 £4.50/hour   2 a £274.50   b 8 hours
3 a £2720   b 8   c £9920
4 After three years: a £15 000   b £14 520
   After six years: a £16 500   b £19 326.12
   Salary **b** if you remain in the job for more than six years, because the total deficit is recovered.

Chapter 9 ARITHMETIC II

Exercise 54 — page 172

1. **a** £278.96 **b** £709.08 **c** £273.96 **d** £381.35
2. £10 215.25
3. **a** £2.63 **b** £39.38 **c** £3.72 **d** £1117.02
4. **a** 'Paint It' **b** 58p **c** £7.83
5. Let £x be cost before VAT is added and £y be the cost after VAT is added. $y = 1.175x$ and $x = \frac{y}{1.175}$, therefore VAT $= \frac{17.5}{100} \times \frac{y}{1.175} = y \times \frac{7}{47}$

Exercise 55 — page 174

1. **a** £20 **b** £150 **c** £421.26 **d** £12 547.21
2. 8 years
3. **a** £1740 **b** (30% is on the amount owing at the start of each year) £1050 **c** £125 **d** £1500
4. **a** £2400 **b** £2250 **c** £19 650

Exercise 56 — page 175

1.

Item	Cost	Selling price at discount of			
		5%	8%	12.5%	15%
Tent	£60	**£57**	**£55.20**	**£52.50**	**£51**
Video	£450	**£427.50**	**£414**	**£393.75**	**£382.50**
Book	£3.50	**£3.33**	**£3.22**	**£3.06**	**£2.98**
Car	£6350	**£6032.50**	**£5842**	**£5556.25**	**£5397.50**

2. £373.64
3. **a** £14.10 **b** £15.79
4. **a** A: £122.40, B: £131.40, therefore A by £9. **b** $9\frac{1}{2}\%$

Revision Exercise 9 — page 176

1.

	Maximum	Minimum	Tolerance
a	10.2	10	0.2
b	8.1	7.9	0.2
c	7.1	6.8	0.3
d	10.01	9	1.01
e	0.91	0.88	0.03
f	≈ 1.15	≈ 1.11	≈ 0.04

2. $A°_{max} \approx 18.4°$, $A°_{min} \approx 15.7°$

Chapter 9 ARITHMETIC II

3 £81 266.54
4 £5 per hour
5 After 3 years: **a** £21 000   **b** £19 360
  After 5 years: **a** £22 000   **b** £23 425.60
  Salary **b** if you remain in the job for more than seven years, because the total deficit is recovered.
6 **a** £306.35   **b** £270.52   **c** £533.92   **d** £677.25
7 £887.77 before marriage, £830.44 after marriage, £57.33 saved per month
8
Item	Before VAT	After VAT
Tie	£12	**£14.10**
Blouse	£32	**£37.60**
Computer	**£578.72**	£680
CD player	**£297.87**	£350

9 **a** £760   **b** £1845   **c** £800
10 **a** £11.25   **b** £58.80   **c** £4131.89   **d** £28 761.22
11 (i) Car   **a** £20 200   **b** £2200
   (ii) TV   **a** £770   **b** £30
   (iii) Skis   **a** £430   **b** £10
   (iv) Bed   **a** £600   **b** £65
12 Top rate of 40%: £32 869.92

Basics Test 5   page 178

A Calculator
  1 0.509
  3 14.9
  5 0.0156
  2 1.66
  4 ± 1.56
  6 5.47

B Paper and pencil
  7 $10\frac{10}{21}$
  9 32 : 24
  11 30 km/h
  13 94 cm²
  15 £21
  8 0.78 kg
  10 0.0150
  12 First
  14 52

Chapter 9 ARITHMETIC II

C Mental
16 What is the value of x minus y? 1
17 What is the value of x cubed? -27
18 Subtract y from minus x. 7
19 Multiply y squared by z. 80
20 What is the value of z to the power of z? 3125

21 What is one eighth as a percentage? 12.5%
22 What is four fifths of ninety? 72
23 Divide a half into point two. 0.4
24 What is the square root of one point six nine? 1.3
25 What is the square root of four point four squared? 4.4

Puzzlers — page 178

1

Red | Red and amber | Green | Amber
a   b   c   d   e → time

$$p(\text{waiting}) = \frac{c-a}{e-a}$$

2 a £388.89   b £532.16   c £729.24

3 Column 3: 1 2 3 4 5 6
                 – – – (*)
                       Y D
                 ─────────
                   C D X Y
                 X B Y D B
                 ─────────
                 X C S Y C Y

Column 3: $C + Y > 9$, since $B \neq C$ in column 2
           Therefore $B + 1 = C$
Column 5: $X + B = C$, therefore $X = 1$
Column 4: $2D = Y$ (first assume no remainder)
Column 6: But $D(*) = Y$ therefore $(*) = 2$
Column 5: $Y(*) = B$ therefore $2Y = B$ (i)
Column 6: $2D = Y$ (ii)
           From (i) and (ii), $Y = 4$
           Therefore $D = 2$, $B = 8$, etc.

Solution: 4 6 0 7
                       4 2
                   ─────────
                   9 2 1 4
                 1 8 4 2 8
                 ─────────
                 1 9 3 4 9 4

Chapter 9 ARITHMETIC II

▬ COURSEWORK: World population   page 179

MARKS (M) 5;   (A) 5;   (E) 3;   (N) 2;   (I) 3;   (C) 2

An interesting and relevant discussion will usually follow this Coursework.

1 After one year the population is 4.6×10^9.
After two years it is 4.7×10^9.
After three years it is 4.8×10^9.
b The population increases by a factor of 1.02 each year.

Years	10	20	30	40	50
Population in billions	5.5	6.7	8.2	9.9	12

The population will double in 35 years.

c

	Year's time	Population	Times larger
(i)	100	3.3×10^{10}	7.2
(ii)	224	3.8×10^{11}	84
(iii)	375	7.6×10^{12}	1700
(iv)	1600	2.6×10^{23}	5.8×10^{13}

2 Total mass = $2.6 \times 10^{23} \times 0.05 = 1.3 \times 10^{22}$ tonnes. This is twice the mass of the Earth. The combined mass of population and Earth remain unchanged.

3 a Total land surface area = $4\pi \times 6350^2 \times 0.3 = 1.5 \times 10^8$ km^2

    b (i) Density at present = $(4.5 \times 10^9) \div (1.5 \times 10^8) = 30$ humans/km^2

       (ii) Density in 100 years = $(3.3 \times 10^{10}) \div (1.5 \times 10^8) = 200$ humans/km^2

       (iii) Density in 224 years = $(3.8 \times 10^{11}) \div (1.5 \times 10^8) = 3000$ humans/km^2

    c (i) 20 m^2 for every one person
       1 m^2 for every $\frac{1}{20}$ person
       1.5×10^{14} for every $\frac{1}{20} \times 1.5 \times 10^{14} = 7.6 \times 10^{12}$ persons
       This is approximately the answer to part 1 c (iii), therefore in 375 years.

       (ii) 20 metres square = 400 m^2
       400 m^2 for every one person
       1 m^2 for every $\frac{1}{400}$ person
       1.5×10^{14} for every $\frac{1}{400} \times 1.5 \times 10^{14} = 3.8 \times 10^{11}$ people
       This is the answer to part 1 c (ii), therefore in 224 years.

4 Disease, famine, war and a changing climate will prevent the population of the world increasing *ad infinitum*. Statistics from China could be collected. Population growth rates included in the report.

Chapter 10 STATISTICS AND PROBABILITY

Activity 33 — page 180

The TV audience trend can be explained by the small number of people (young children and mothers) at home during the day whilst the upturn at 4 pm is due to the returning population of school children. The sharp increase in viewers at 6 pm is a result of the returning working population. The downturn after about 10 pm is obviously due to people going to bed!
The radio audience peaks in the morning and tails off in the evening because many people do not enjoy daytime TV and some employees are able to listen to the radio whilst at work.
About 150% more people watch TV than listen to the radio. The 65+ age group watch 38 hours of TV per week, as they are by nature less active than other age groups.
The amount of sport shown in the period 1987–88 was more than between 1981–82 (why?).

Activity 34 — page 182

A percentage comparison may also be a useful revision exercise.

Activity 35 — page 182

a This sample would consist largely of housewives. It could be improved by collecting opinions from different age groups and 'types' from different locations at different times.
b This sample generally consisted of wealthy people as only these could afford telephones in the 1940s and their voting intentions were biased. It could have been improved by using the same technique as described in **a**.
c This is not a random sample and could be disastrous. For example, the faults may occur every twentieth or even every twentyfifth fridge! It could be improved by allocating every fridge with a number and selecting these for inspection by use of a random number generator.
d Clearly the opinions will be in favour of Nottingham Forest FC. It could have been improved by using the same technique as described in **a**.

Activity 36 — page 183

The volume of the boys' 'block' is **not** twice that of the girls'.
Useful sources are advertisements from newspapers, TV or radio.

Exercise 57 — page 184

1 b Approximately 7   **2 b** Approximately 60 mm
3 a

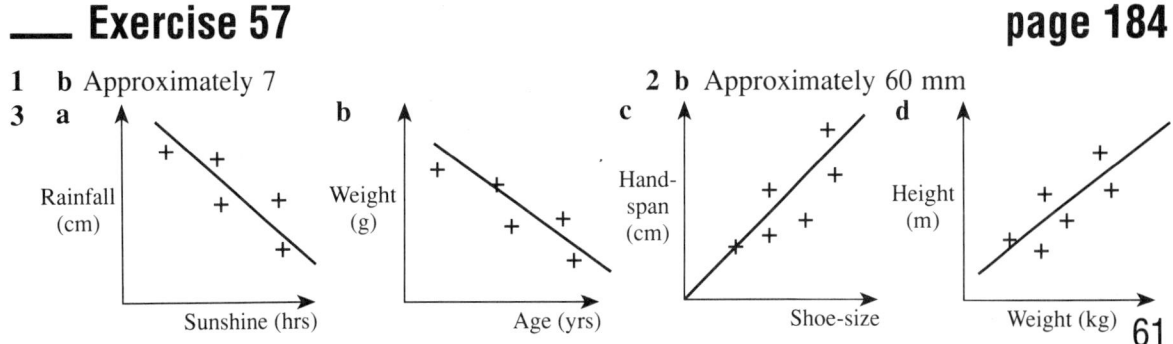

Chapter 10 STATISTICS AND PROBABILITY

— Activity 37   page 185

The trisection error increases with line length.

— Exercise 58   page 187

1 a (i) 10 (ii) 12 (iii) 14   b (i) 15 (ii) 16 (iii) 4   c (i) 1.25 (ii) 1.0 (iii) –
2 a 49.8%   b (49.8 + 10)%
3 Mean = 92, median = 91, mode = 91, therefore median or mode.
4 a 2.8   b 3   c 2; mode   5 10.5   a 108.5   b 54.25
6 10.5
7 Mean_{min} = £12.60. Mean_{max} = £14.40. Therefore £12.50 is not possible
8 231°, 232°   9 7.9
10 a 60   b 62

— Activity 38   page 188

1 Modal class is tallest bar, that is, most frequency.
2 Where a clip is bent, speed of bending, angle of bending, etc.
3 You should expect a distribution approaching the shape of the normal distribution.

— Activity 39   page 189

3 A symmetrical triangular distribution.

— Exercise 59   page 189

1 a 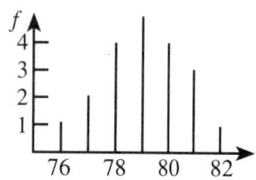   b Yes, as few would score very low
                                     or very high.
                                   c 79

2 a

Matches	f
47	2
49	2
50	2
51	2
52	2

b Mean = 49.8, therefore yes (just).

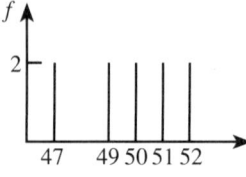

Chapter 10 STATISTICS AND PROBABILITY

3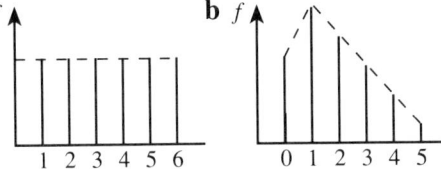

4 A typical comparison might be: 'books' are skewed to right, 'comics' are skewed to left. Therefore comics use shorter words than books.

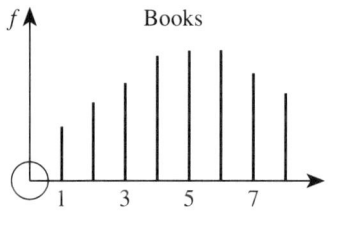 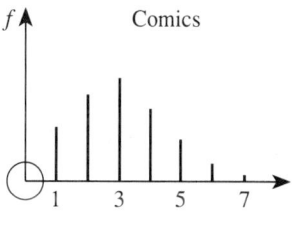

── Activity 40 — page 191

3 You should expect a distribution approaching the shape of the normal distribution.

── Exercise 60 — page 192

1 Modal class is 17.5–20.5 minutes.

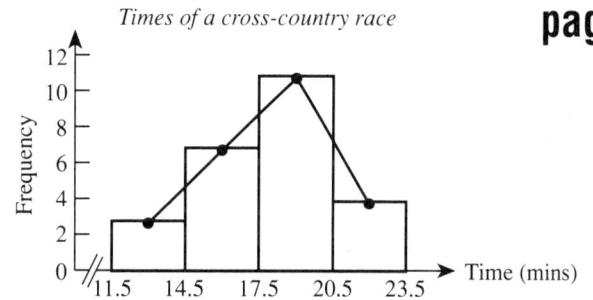

2 Modal class is 22–28 years.

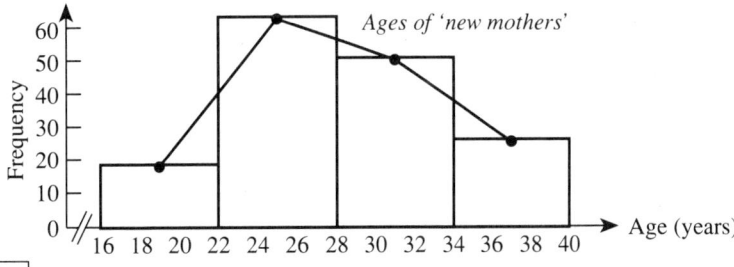

3 a

Class (cm)	Frequency
165–170	9
170–175	5
175–180	10
180–185	5
185–190	3

b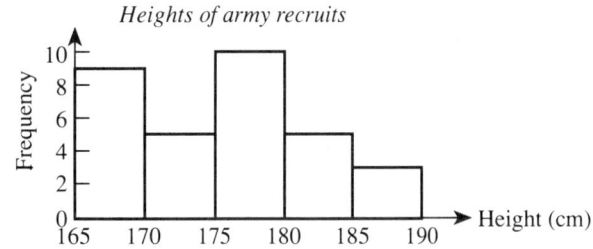

c Modal class is 175–180 cm.

Chapter 10 STATISTICS AND PROBABILITY

4   Overall, the low sales in 1990 rose considerably in 1991 (almost doubled)

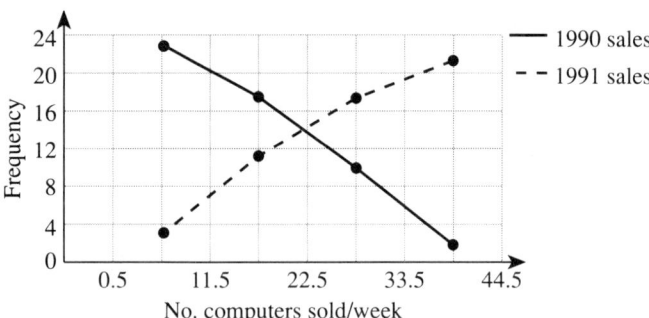

___ Activity 41   page 194

2   $p(A) + p(\overline{A}) = 1$

___ Activity 42   page 195

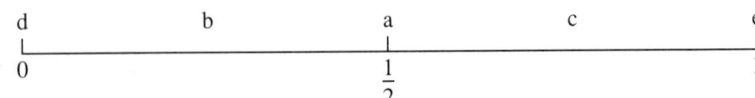

___ Exercise 61   page 196

1   a $\frac{1}{6}$ b $\frac{1}{2}$ c $\frac{1}{2}$ d $\frac{1}{3}$

2   a $\frac{1}{4}$ b $\frac{1}{2}$

50p	T	H	T	H
20p	T	H	H	T

3   a $\frac{1}{2}$ b $\frac{1}{13}$ c $\frac{3}{13}$ d $\frac{3}{13}$
4   a $\frac{1}{3}$ b $\frac{1}{2}$ c 0
5   a $\frac{3}{10}$ b $\frac{2}{5}$ c $\frac{3}{10}$
6   a $\frac{1}{6}$ b $\frac{1}{3}$ c $\frac{1}{3}$

7

		Die					
		1	2	3	4	5	6
Coin	T	*	*	*	*	*	*
	H	*	*	*	*	*	*

a $\frac{1}{12}$
b $\frac{1}{4}$
c 0

8   a $\frac{3}{50}$ b $\frac{2}{25}$
9   The statement means that half the people who live to 105 survive to their 106th birthday!

Chapter 10 STATISTICS AND PROBABILITY

10

		\multicolumn{6}{c}{Red}					
		1	2	3	4	5	6
	1	2	3	4	5	6	7
	2	3	4	5	6	7	8
	3	4	5	6	7	8	9
Black	4	5	6	7	8	9	10
	5	6	7	8	9	10	11
	6	7	8	9	10	11	12

a (i) $\frac{5}{36}$ (ii) $\frac{1}{36}$
(iii) $\frac{1}{12}$ (iv) $\frac{1}{12}$
b 7

11

		\multicolumn{6}{c}{Red}					
		1	2	3	4	5	6
	1	1	2	3	4	5	6
	2	2	4	6	8	10	12
	3	3	6	9	12	15	18
Black	4	4	8	12	16	20	24
	5	5	10	15	20	25	30
	6	6	12	18	24	30	36

a (i) $\frac{1}{12}$ (ii) $\frac{3}{4}$
(iii) $\frac{1}{9}$ (iv) $\frac{25}{36}$
b 6 or 12

Activity 43   page 198

3

		\multicolumn{6}{c}{RH die}					
		1	2	3	4	5	6
	1	XX	X$\overline{\text{X}}$	X$\overline{\text{X}}$	X$\overline{\text{X}}$	X$\overline{\text{X}}$	X$\overline{\text{X}}$
	2	$\overline{\text{X}}$X	$\overline{\text{XX}}$	$\overline{\text{XX}}$	$\overline{\text{XX}}$	$\overline{\text{XX}}$	$\overline{\text{XX}}$
	3	$\overline{\text{X}}$X	$\overline{\text{XX}}$	$\overline{\text{XX}}$	$\overline{\text{XX}}$	$\overline{\text{XX}}$	$\overline{\text{XX}}$
LH die	4	$\overline{\text{X}}$X	$\overline{\text{XX}}$	$\overline{\text{XX}}$	$\overline{\text{XX}}$	$\overline{\text{XX}}$	$\overline{\text{XX}}$
	5	$\overline{\text{X}}$X	$\overline{\text{XX}}$	$\overline{\text{XX}}$	$\overline{\text{XX}}$	$\overline{\text{XX}}$	$\overline{\text{XX}}$
	6	$\overline{\text{X}}$X	$\overline{\text{XX}}$	$\overline{\text{XX}}$	$\overline{\text{XX}}$	$\overline{\text{XX}}$	$\overline{\text{XX}}$

a $\frac{1}{36}$
b $\frac{5}{36}$
c $\frac{5}{36}$
d $\frac{25}{36}$
e $\frac{13}{18}$
f $\frac{5}{18}$

4 The experimental results of the whole class should be closer to the theoretical answers than to an individual's results.

Exercise 62   page 201

1 **a** $\frac{1}{36}$ **b** $\frac{25}{36}$ **c** $\frac{5}{36}$ **d** $\frac{5}{18}$
2 **a** $\frac{4}{25}$ **b** $\frac{9}{25}$ **c** $\frac{6}{25}$ **d** $\frac{12}{25}$
3 **a** $\frac{4}{25}$ **b** $\frac{9}{25}$ **c** $\frac{6}{25}$ **d** $\frac{12}{25}$
4 **a** $\frac{4}{9}$ **b** $\frac{4}{9}$ **c** $\frac{1}{9}$
5 **a** $\frac{1}{50}$ **b** $\frac{4}{50}$ **c** $\frac{18}{25}$
6 $\frac{2}{15}$

Chapter 10 STATISTICS AND PROBABILITY

Exercise 63   page 202

1 a $\frac{1}{21}$ b $\frac{10}{21}$ c $\frac{20}{21}$
2 a $\frac{1}{9}$ b $\frac{4}{9}$ c $\frac{5}{9}$
3 a $\frac{1}{6}$ b $\frac{5}{18}$ c $\frac{13}{18}$
4 a $\frac{1}{27}$ b $\frac{2}{9}$ c $\frac{7}{27}$
5 a $\frac{1}{8}$ b $\frac{3}{8}$ c $\frac{1}{2}$ d $\frac{7}{8}$
6 a $\frac{2}{9}$ b $\frac{8}{45}$ c $\frac{2}{45}$ d $\frac{43}{45}$
7 a $\frac{1}{5}$ b $\frac{3}{7}$ c $\frac{1}{5}$ d $\frac{4}{5}$
8 Events 'King' and 'Heart' are not independent, for example there is a King of Hearts.
9 a $\frac{5}{72}$ b $\frac{5}{12}$ c $\frac{91}{216}$

Activity 44   page 204

1 As N is increased the approximation for π improves.
2 As N is increased the distribution becomes more symmetrically triangular.

Revision Exercise 10   page 205

1 a 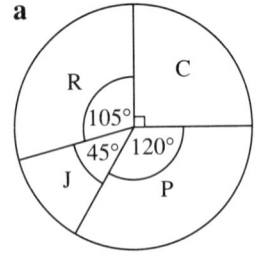   b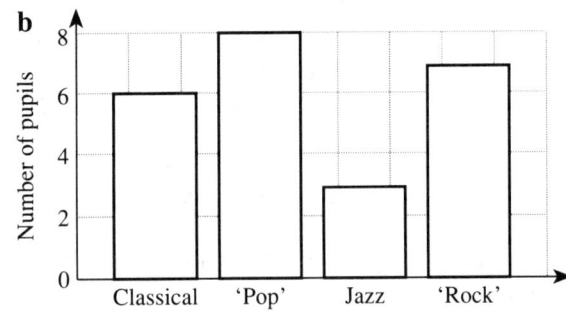

2 a Football boots: £2400
   b Running shoes: £3000
   c Tennis rackets: £1000
   d Track suits: £1600
3 a 19 words/min, 20 words/min, 21 words/min
   b 20 words/min, 21 words/min, 23 words/min
   c $19\frac{1}{3}$ words/min, 20 words/min, 21 words/min
4 93%
5 b Approximately 49 seconds
6 Modal class is 100–120 g. Approximately two thirds of the apples are heavier than 100 g.

Masses of 150 apples

Chapter 10 STATISTICS AND PROBABILITY

7 a (Slight skew towards the higher amount of money.)

Class (p)	Frequency
20–30	3
30–40	2
40–50	4
50–60	1
60–70	3
70–80	6
80–90	4
90–100	1

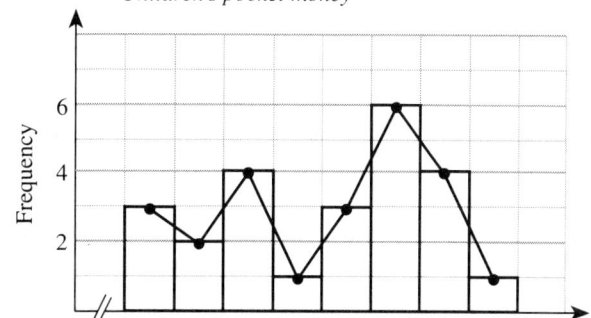

Children's pocket money

8 a $p(a) = \frac{7}{51}$ **b** $p(t) = \frac{1}{17}$ **c** $p(\text{vowel}) = \frac{1}{3}$ **d** $p(x) = 0$

9

		1st spin				
		1	2	3	4	5
2nd spin	1	2	3	4	5	6
	2	3	4	5	6	7
	3	4	5	6	7	8
	4	5	6	7	8	9
	5	6	7	8	9	10

a $p(\text{sum} = 4) = \frac{3}{25}$
b $p(\text{sum} = 6) = \frac{1}{5}$
c $p(\text{sum} = 11) = 0$
d $p(\text{sum} \geq 7) = \frac{2}{5}$
e $p(\text{sum} < 5) = \frac{6}{25}$
Assumed the spinner is fair.

10 a $p(\text{no goals}) = \frac{25}{49}$ **b** $p(1; \text{goal in each of two matches}) = \frac{4}{49}$ **c** $p(1; \text{goal}) = \frac{20}{49}$

11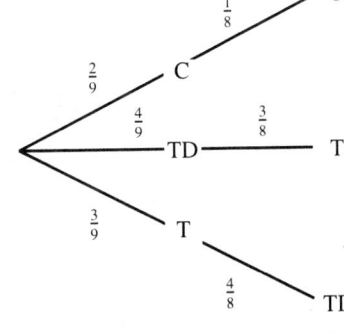

a $p(2C) = \frac{1}{36}$
b $p(\text{TD, T}) = \frac{1}{6}$
c $p(\text{TD, T}) = \frac{1}{6}$
Therefore $p(\text{TD, T } or \text{ T, TD}) = \frac{1}{6} + \frac{1}{6} = \frac{1}{3}$
e x: number of caramels
$p(x \geq 1) = 1 - p(x < 1)$
$= 1 - p(x = 0)$
$= 1 - \frac{7}{9} \times \frac{6}{8}$
$= 1 - \frac{42}{72} = \frac{5}{12}$

12 a $p(B) = \frac{17}{30}$ **b** $p(W) = \frac{13}{30}$

Aural Test 3   page 207

1. What is the area of a rectangular room measuring three point nine metres by two point eight metres?   10.92 m²
2. Subtract six pounds fifty eight from fifteen pounds twenty three.   £8.65
3. What is the cost of nine bars of chocolate if seven cost two pounds forty five?   £3.15

(*Continued*)

Chapter 10 STATISTICS AND PROBABILITY

4 A television programme started at thirteen forty nine and finished at fifteen sixteen. How many minutes did it last? 87
5 Mary walks four miles at an average speed of five miles per hour. For how many minutes did she walk? 48 minutes
6 The asking price for a house is ninety eight thousand pounds. If it is sold for ten per cent less, what was it sold for? £88 200
7 How many twenty four pence stamps could Mrs Shah buy for ten pounds? 41
8 Pluto is six thousand million kilometres from Earth. Write this distance in standard form. 6×10^9 km
9 What is the average of all the counting numbers between ninety and one hundred inclusive? 95
10 Divide seventy two pounds in the ratio of four to five. £32, £40
11 What is the mode? 2 goals
12 What is the total number of goals scored? 44
13 What is the average number of goals scored per match? 2.2 goals
14 In how many matches were more than two goals scored? 8
15 How many more times expensive is it to make a call at Peak Rate than at Cheap Rate? 6 times
16 For how long could you make a call at Standard Rate for fifty pence? 15 minutes
17 How much would a weekday three minute call cost at nine am? 15p
18 What is the maximum length of call you could make for one pound? 2 hours
19 Which of the speeds shown is approximately equal to ten miles per hour? 5 m/s
20 The square root of twelve million is approximately which of the numbers shown? 3600

___ Puzzlers   page 207

1 One end is tied to a fixed post. A pupil stands a certain distance from the post. The string is wound around pupil and post. The pupil then moves, either towards or away from the post until there are exactly ten lengths between them.

2 Any answer is correct. The wires will always cross at the same height above the deck and the perpendicular distance to each mast is always in the ratio 2 : 3. Pupils should demonstrate these results by scale drawing.

3 T is the centre of gravity of the triangle ABC.

4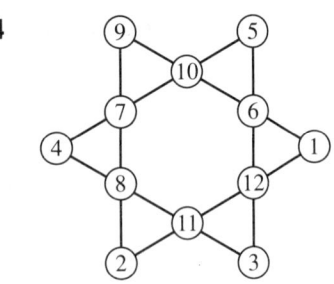

Chapter 10 STATISTICS AND PROBABILITY

5 (i) Draw any angle ABC. Produce CB to D. Draw any circle centre B, to meet BA at Y, BC at X and BD at Z. Place two marks on a ruler, Q and P, where PQ = radius of circle drawn.
(ii) Place the ruler so that P lies on DZ, Q lies on the circle and that it also passes through Y. Draw line PQY.
(iii) Join QB. Let QPZ = $x°$, therefore BQY = $2x°$, and YBX = $3x°$. Finally translate angle QPX from P to B, by sliding the ruler along.

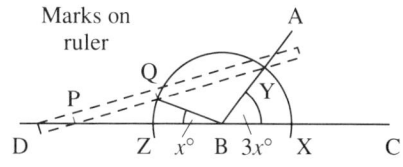

6 Let r = radius of earth. Using similar triangles: $\frac{r}{162.5+r} = \frac{1410}{1410.036}$
Therefore r = 6360 km to 3 SF.

___ COURSEWORK: Traffic flow problem   page 208

MARKS (M) 4; (A) 5; (E) 4; (N) 2; (I) 2; (C) 3

One die per two pupils is required for this Coursework.

1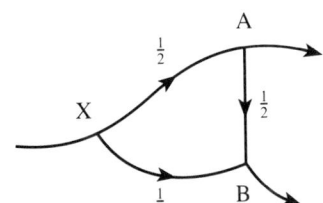

a $p(A) = \frac{1}{2}$
  $p(B) = \frac{1}{2} + \left(\frac{1}{2} \times \frac{1}{2}\right) = \frac{3}{4}$
b Vehicles passing:
  (i) A = 30
  (ii) B = 45
  (iii) B not via A = 30

2 a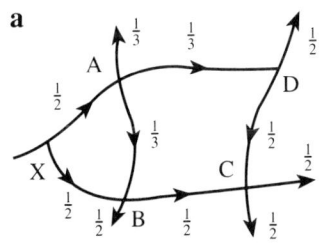

b (i) $p(A) = \frac{1}{2}$
  (ii) $p(B) = \frac{1}{2} + \left(\frac{1}{2} \times \frac{1}{3}\right) = \frac{2}{3}$
  (iii) $p(C) = (\frac{1}{2} \times \frac{1}{3} \times \frac{1}{2}) + (\frac{1}{2} \times \frac{1}{3} \times \frac{1}{2}) + (\frac{1}{2} \times \frac{1}{2})$
    $= \frac{5}{12}$
  (iv) $p(D) = \frac{1}{2} \times \frac{1}{3} = \frac{1}{6}$
c Vehicles passing:
  (i) A = 30   (ii) B = 40
  (iii) C = 25   (iv) D = 10

3 Note that pupils are **not** asked to record simulated traffic flow out of the network. For example, at 'A' if a '5' or '6' is rolled, the car leaves the system and is not recorded.
a A brief explanation is required together with the completed Table 2.
b A clearly labelled bar chart showing practical results and the theoretical results (A = 30, B = 40, C = 25, D = 10).

Comments: percentages could be used to compare the theoretical and practical results. The difference would be less if the simulation were larger than 60.

Chapter 10 STATISTICS AND PROBABILITY

4 *First proposal*

$p(C) = (\frac{1}{2} \times \frac{1}{3} \times \frac{1}{2}) + (\frac{1}{2} \times \frac{1}{3} \times \frac{1}{3}) + (\frac{1}{2} \times \frac{1}{3})$
$+ (\frac{1}{2} \times \frac{1}{3} \times \frac{1}{3} \times \frac{1}{2}) + (\frac{1}{2} \times \frac{1}{3} \times \frac{1}{2})$
$= \frac{15}{36} = \frac{5}{12}$

Therefore vehicles/hour $= \frac{5}{12} \times 3600 = 1500$

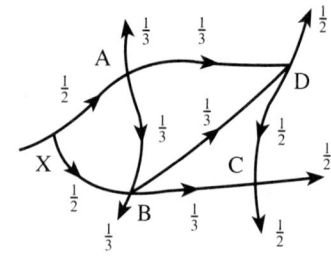

Second proposal

$p(C) = (\frac{1}{2} \times \frac{1}{3} \times \frac{1}{2}) + (\frac{1}{2} \times \frac{1}{2}) = \frac{4}{12} = \frac{1}{3}$

Therefore vehicles/hour $= \frac{1}{3} \times 3600 = 1200$.

The second proposal would fulfil the design requirements.

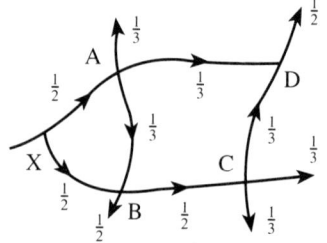

If your pupils are keen and able to write a short computer program to simulate traffic flow for part 3, the following program in BBC Basic may be of use.

```
10    REM: "CAR"-Traffic Coursework
20    :
30    A=0:B=0:C=0:D=0:CAR=0
40    REPEAT:CAR=CAR+1:P$="X":REPEAT
50    IFP$="X":PROCX
60    IFP$="A":PROCA
70    IFP$="B":PROCB
80    IFP$="C":PROCC
90    IFP$="D":PROCD
100   UNTILP$="E":UNTILCAR=60
110   :
120   PRINT"CAR=";CAR:PRINT" A=";A:PRINT" B=";B:PRINT" C=";C:PRINT" D=";D
130   PRINT"Another go? Y/N";:G$=GET$:VDU13,15:PRINTSPC16
140   IFG$="Y"ORG$="Y$" RUN:ELSE END
150   :
160   DEFPROCX:X=RND(6):IFX=1 OR X=3 OR X=5:P$="A":ELSEP$="B"
170   ENDPROC
180   DEFPROCA:A=A+1:X=RND(6)
190   IFX=1 OR X=2 P$="B":ELSEIFX=3 OR X=4 P$="D":ELSEP$="E"
200   ENDPROC
210   DEFPROCB:B=B+1:X=RND(6)
220   IFX=1 OR X=3 OR X=5:P$="C":ELSEP$="E"
230   ENDPROC
240   DEFPROCC:C=C+1:P$="E";ENDPROC
250   DEFPROCD:D=D+1:X=RND(6)
260   IFX=2 OR X=4 OR X=6:P$="C":ELSEP$="E"
270   ENDPROC
```

Chapter 11 GEOMETRY II

Exercise 64   page 212

1 A (6, 0), (5, 2), (4, 0)   B (2, −5), (1, −3), (0, −5)
C (5, 4), (4, 6), (3, 4)   D (−4, 3), (−5, 5), (−6, 3)
E (1, −6), (0, −4), (−1, −6)   F (−3, −2), (−4, 0), (−5, −2)

2 A $\binom{6}{2}$ B $\binom{4}{4}$ C $\binom{-4}{4}$ D $\binom{-8}{0}$ E $\binom{-8}{-2}$ F $\binom{-7}{-4}$ G $\binom{0}{-6}$ H $\binom{6}{-6}$

3

	Object	Reflection in line	Image
a	A	$x = 5$	B
b	F	$x = 5$	G
c	G	**$x = 5$**	F
d	A	$x = 7$	C
e	D	**$x = 12$**	B
f	G	$x = 9$	H
g	K	**$x = 24$**	J
h	I	$x = 12$	G
i	**H or K**	$x = 18$	**K or H**
j	E	$x = 10$	A
k	J	**$x = 15$**	G
l	**D or E**	$x = 17$	**E or D**

a (189, 3), (189, 5), (189, 7), (191, 6)
b $(2a − 13, 3)$, $(2a − 13, 5)$, $(2a − 13, 7)$, $(2a − 11, 6)$

4 **c** $y = -x$

5

Object	Rotation centre	angle	Image
B	(0, −2)	90° anticlockwise	D
A	(1, −2)	180°	D
D	**(0, −2)**	**90° clockwise**	B
G	(1, −1)	90° anticlockwise	I
F	**(−3, −3)**	**90° anticlockwise**	I
I	(−3, −3)	**90° clockwise**	F
C	(0, 2.5)	**180°**	G
D	(−1, −4)	**90° anticlockwise**	F
H	(3, 1)	**90° anticlockwise**	D
D	(−3, 0)	90° anticlockwise	G
I	(−1.5, −2.5)	**180°**	D
H or G	(−0.5, 3.5)	**180°**	**G or H**
C	**(2.5, −0.5)**	90° anticlockwise	D

6 **a** (2, −3)   **b** (−2, 3)   **c** (−3, −2)   **d** (61, −16), (−61, 16), (−16, −61)

Chapter 11 GEOMETRY II

7 e R onto T: translation $\begin{pmatrix} 4 \\ 6 \end{pmatrix}$

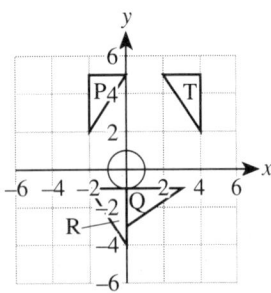

8 e S onto U: rotation 180° about (0, 0)

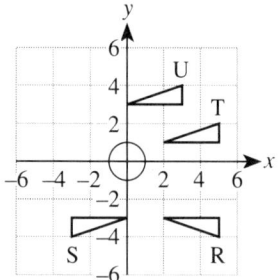

▬ Activity 45 page 216

1 a $\frac{CX'}{CX} = \frac{CY'}{CY} = \frac{CZ'}{CZ} = 2$. These ratios are all equal, hence △XYZ is similar to △X'Y'Z'.
  b Scale factor of enlargement = 2   **c** Area △XYZ:Area △X'Y'Y' = 1 : 2² = 1 : 4
2 a $\frac{OQ'}{OQ} = \frac{OR'}{OR} = \frac{OP'}{OP} = \frac{2}{3}$. Hence △PQR is similar to △P'Q'R'.
  b Scale factor of enlargement = $\frac{2}{3}$ **c** Area △PQR:Area △P'Q'R' = 1 : $\left(\frac{2}{3}\right)^2$ = 1 : $\frac{4}{9}$ = 9 : 4

▬ Exercise 65 page 217

1 a P' (−4, −2), Q' (−2, −2), R' (−4, +2)   **b** P' (0, −3), Q' (1$\frac{1}{2}$, −3), R' (0, 0)
  c P' (1, −1), Q' (3$\frac{1}{2}$, −1), R' (1, 4)   **d** P' (−2, 2), Q' (−1, 2), R' (−2, 4)
2 a L' (3$\frac{1}{2}$, 0), M' (3$\frac{1}{2}$, −3$\frac{1}{2}$), N' (0, −3$\frac{1}{2}$)   **b** L' (−2, 4$\frac{1}{2}$), M' (−2, 2), N' (−4$\frac{1}{2}$, 2)
  c L' (−$\frac{1}{2}$, −1), M' (−$\frac{1}{2}$, −2$\frac{1}{2}$), N' (−2, −2$\frac{1}{2}$)   **d** L' (2$\frac{1}{2}$, 3), M' (2$\frac{1}{2}$, $\frac{1}{2}$), N' (0, $\frac{1}{2}$)
3 a E' (−$\frac{1}{2}$, $\frac{1}{2}$), F' ($\frac{1}{2}$, 2$\frac{1}{2}$), D' ($\frac{1}{2}$, −$\frac{1}{2}$)   **b** E' (−2, 0), F' (−1, 2), D' (−1, −1)
  c E' (0, 0), F' (1$\frac{1}{2}$, 3), D' (1$\frac{1}{2}$, −1$\frac{1}{2}$)   **d** E' (−1$\frac{1}{2}$, −3), F' (−1, −2), D' (−1, −3$\frac{1}{2}$)
4 a R' (0, −4), S' (−2, −4), T' (−4, 0)   **b** R' (1, 0), S' ($\frac{1}{2}$, 0), T' (0, 1)
  c R' (1, −1), S' ($\frac{1}{2}$, −1), T' (0, 0)   **d** R' (3$\frac{3}{4}$, 0), S' (2$\frac{1}{4}$, 0), T' ($\frac{3}{4}$, 3)
5 a 2.5 **b** 1$\frac{2}{3}$ **c** $\frac{2}{5}$ **d** $\frac{3}{5}$ **e** $\frac{2}{3}$ **f** 1$\frac{1}{2}$
6 a A to B: (i) SF = 0.8 (ii) % reduction = 20%. B to C: (i) SF = 0.75 (ii) % reduction = 25%.
  b 1:1500
7 a 2.4 **b** 7.2 cm **c** Scale factors are ratios of the corresponding sides of the image to the object.
8 Centre (3.8, 4.6). SF = −3.7

▬ Activity 46 page 219

1  2 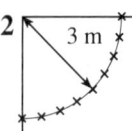 3 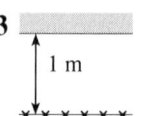 4 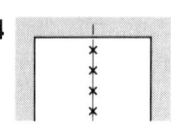 5  6 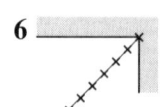 7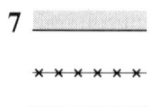

Chapter 11 GEOMETRY II

Exercise 66 — page 220

1 1a in the pupils' book should read '5 cm from A'.

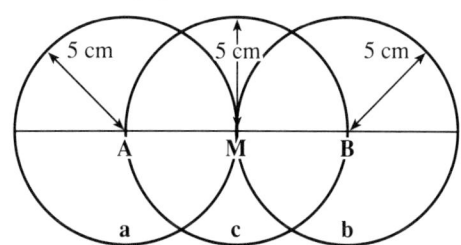

2

(circle with 6 cm radius, points P, M, Q, labels a, b, c)

3

(circle with 4 cm radius, points X, M, Y, labels a, b, c)

4 a Arc of a circle parallel to the floor.
   b An inclined line parallel and above the line of the bannister rail.
   c A cycloid.

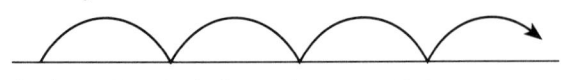

   d Arc of a circle in a plane parallel to the table top.

5 575 ± 5 m
7 162 ± 3 m
8 86 ± 2 m (there is only 1 point)
9 The shape formed is called an 'ellipse'.

6

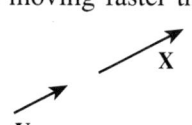

10 The centre of gravity is the intersection of the lines which join the mid points of each side to the opposite vertex. The centre of gravity is always one third of the way along each line.

Activity 47 — page 223

1 b 2 cm represents 1 km, therefore 1 cm represents 0.5 km, therefore scale is 1 : 50 000.
   c (i) 533246 (ii) A: 4.75 cm = 2.375 km   B: 7.2 cm = 3.6 km   (iii) 333°
2 b 4 cm represents 1 km, therefore 1 cm represents 0.25 km, therefore scale is 1 : 25 000.
   d In part 2 the area of map is four times greater, therefore greater accuracy can be obtained.

Exercise 67 — page 223

1 a 509228   b 341°   c XY = 9.5 cm ≈ 4.75 km
2 a 529235   b 2.9 km   c 1 hour 27 minutes
3 2 km from 520235 in any direction.   **4** a 10.8 km   b 5.0 km²   c 519237
5 The exceptions are:
   a Parallel courses   b Opposite directions   c Same direction but X is moving faster than Y   d

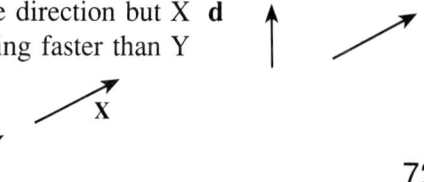

73

Chapter 11 GEOMETRY II

6

Route	Distance (km) to 4 SF	Time to nearest second	Bearing to follow to nearest degree
S to A	2.236	11 m 11 s	207°
A to C	2.062	10 m 19 s	256°
C to B	1.803	9 m 1 s	034°
B to G	1.118	5 m 35 s	333°
G to F	3.162	15 m 49 s	342°
F to E	3.202	16 m 1 s	141°
E to D	0.7071	3 m 32 s	045°
D to S	1.414	7 m 4 s	135°
Totals	15.70	1 h 18 m 32 s	*

The above figures do not take into account terrain, fatigue or weather. The bearings are grid bearings and would have to be converted into magnetic bearings before they could be used on the ground.

━━ Activity 48   page 225

You may like to point out that the inclinometer's height should be taken into account when estimating heights!

━━ Exercise 68   page 226

1   **a** 153 m   **b** 68 m   **c** 28 m
   A diagonal has to be included because of the principle of 'triangulation'.
2   **a** 102 m
3   **a** 24.5 km   **b** 60 km/h
4   **a** 4.82 m/s   **b** Fielder's time = 2.1 s. Ball's time = 2.8 s. Therefore yes.

━━ Exercise 69   page 228

1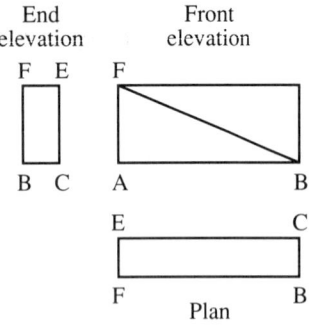

2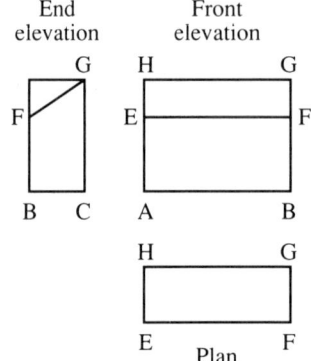

3

Chapter 11 GEOMETRY II

4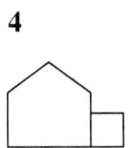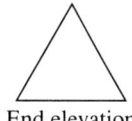
Front elevation 3 dimensional

5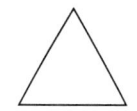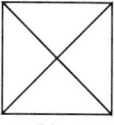
3 dimensional End elevation Front elevation Plan

	Front elevation	End elevation	3-dimensional
6a			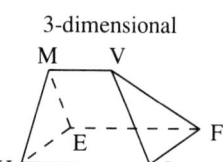
b	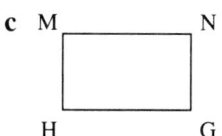	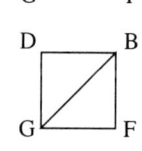	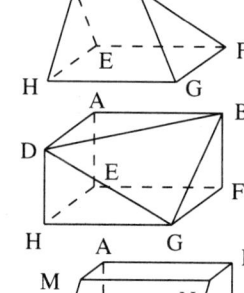
c	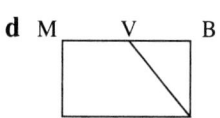	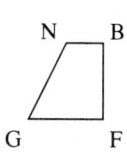	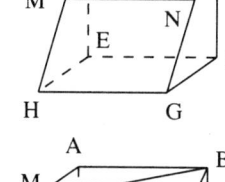
d		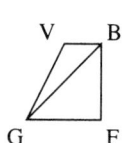	

Exercise 70 — page 230

1 2, even **2** 4, even **3** 3, odd **4** 4, even
5 3, odd **6** 4, even **7** 2, even **8** 3, odd
9 2, even **10** 3, odd **11** 1, odd **12** 3, odd
13 6, even **14** 2, even

Activity 49 — page 230

1

	Even nodes	Odd nodes	Traversable		Even nodes	Odd nodes	Traversable
a	1	0	Yes	e	2	2	Yes
b	2	2	Yes	f	0	4	No
c	1	4	No	g	10	0	Yes
d	0	4	No	h	1	6	No

2 If a network is traversable, the number of odd nodes is 0 or 2.

Chapter 11 GEOMETRY II

3
4

	Traversable	Starting point	Finishing point	R	N	A
a	No	–	–	5	5	8
b	Yes	P	R	5	3	6
c	Yes	M	N	5	2	5
d	No	–	–	5	6	9
e	Yes	T	R	3	3	4
f	Yes	H	K	4	4	6
g	Yes	F	D	3	4	5
h	No	–	–	4	4	6
i	No	–	–	5	3	6
j	No	–	–	4	4	6
k	No	–	–	4	6	8
l	Yes	D	D	7	4	9
m	Yes	U	W	4	3	5
n	No	–	–	4	6	8
o	No	–	–	5	4	7
p	Yes	K	J	4	7	9

    b $R + N = A + 2$

5   **a** 5   **b** 11   **c** 5   **d** 8   **e** 4   **f** 5   **g** 2

6   Possible: a, e. Impossible: b, c, d.

Exercise 71   page 235

All programs should begin with:

L	RM
ST ↵	CL ↵
HOME ↵	CT ↵

These answers are for the Logotron version of LOGO.

1 FD 150 ↵
    RT 90 ↵
    FD 150 ↵
    RT 90 ↵
    FD 150 ↵
    RT 90 ↵
    FD 150 ↵
    RT 90 ↵

2 FD 150 ↵
    RT 90 ↵
    FD 300 ↵
    RT 90 ↵
    FD 150 ↵
    RT 90 ↵
    FD 300 ↵
    RT 90 ↵

3 RT 30 ↵
    FD 200 ↵
    RT 120 ↵
    FD 200 ↵
    RT 120 ↵
    FD 200 ↵

Chapter 11 GEOMETRY II

4 RT 25 ↵
    FD 142 ↵
    RT 65 ↵
    FD 156 ↵
    RT 115 ↵
    FD 142 ↵
    RT 65 ↵
    FD 156 ↵

5 TO HEX ↵
    REPEAT 6 [FD 135 RT 60] ↵
    END ↵

6 TO PENT ↵
    REPEAT 5 [FD 140 RT 72] ↵
    END ↵

7 a FD 200 ↵
    RT 90 ↵
    FD 300 ↵
    RT 90 ↵
    FD 150 ↵
    RT 90 ↵
    FD 150 ↵

b RT 90 ↵
    FD 400 ↵
    RT 120 ↵
    FD 300 ↵
    RT 150 ↵
    FD 500 ↵
    RT 90 ↵
    FD 300 ↵

c FD 200 ↵
    RT 120 ↵
    FD 100 ↵
    RT 120 ↵
    FD 200 ↵
    LT 120 ↵
    FD 100 ↵

d TO TRI ↵
    RT 22.5 ↵
    FD 130.7 ↵
    LT 112.5 ↵
    FD 100 ↵
    LT 112.5 ↵
    FD 130.7 ↵
    LT 157.5 ↵
    END ↵
    TO OCTAGON ↵
    REPEAT 8 [TRI RT 45] ↵
    END ↵

Revision Exercise 11

page 236

1 a to **d**
  e S onto P: reflection in $y = 1$

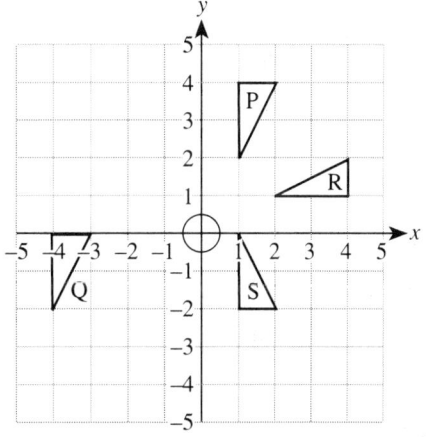

2 a Translation of $\begin{pmatrix} -4 \\ -6 \end{pmatrix}$
  b Reflection in $y = x$
  c Reflection in $y = 2$
  d Rotation 180° about (4, 0)
  e Rotation 90° anti-clockwise about $(-3, -3)$
  f Rotation 90° clockwise about (2, 2)

4

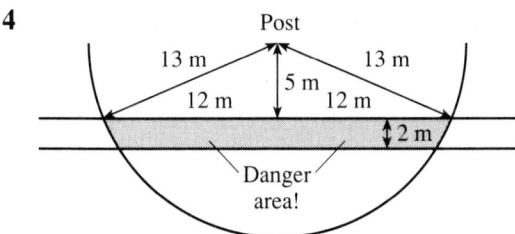

5 Assuming zero thickness of walls and swivel chair at A, all but 4.75% of the playground can be seen.

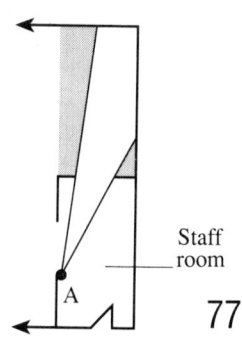

Chapter 11 GEOMETRY II

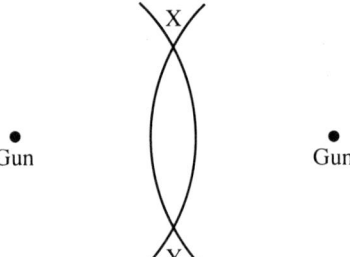

6 See diagram. The shortest route is a straight line from X to Y but this would be in the range of both guns. A safer route might be to travel along one of the arcs, just outside of the range of one of the guns.

7 a 9.9 km **b** 3.3 km/h to 2 SF **c** 4 km²

8 a $R = 3, N = 3, A = 4$ **b** $R = 5, N = 3, A = 6$
c $R = 5, N = 3, A = 6$

9 a 16:55 **b** 15:04 bearing = 010°

___ Basic Algebra Test 3   page 238

1   2
2   $3x^3$
3   $9y^3$
4   $1\frac{1}{2}y$

5   $\frac{3}{x^2} + 1$
6   $\frac{c}{2}$
7   $\frac{r+s}{rs}$
8   $\frac{t-1}{t}$

9   $\frac{2a^2}{3}$
10   $\frac{4}{9}$
11   $8x^4$
12   1

13   9
14   -9
15   9
16   9

17   $x = y(m + b)$
18   $x = \frac{p}{q} + a$
19   $x = a - b$
20   $x = \frac{a}{m-2}$

21   $x(x^2 + x - 1)$
22   $2x^2 y^2 (x - 2y)$
23   $x > \frac{3}{5}$
24   $x \leq 1$

25   $\frac{-x-3}{x(x+1)}$
26   -1
27   $x = \pm \sqrt{\frac{c-b}{a}}$
28   $\frac{ac-a}{c}$

29   $\pm 1\frac{1}{2}$
30   -2
31   12 or -16
32   -2 or 3

___ Puzzlers   page 238

1 $m = 2t + 1.\ m = 1001,\ t = 500$

2 $a = 13,\ b = 11.\ a^2 + b^2 = 290$

3

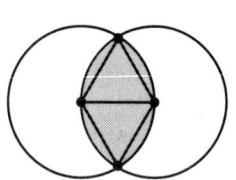

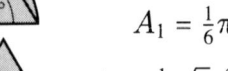 $A_1 = \frac{1}{6}\pi r^2$

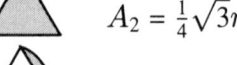 $A_2 = \frac{1}{4}\sqrt{3} r^2$

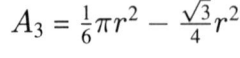 $A_3 = \frac{1}{6}\pi r^2 - \frac{\sqrt{3}}{4} r^2$

$A = 2\left(\frac{1}{6}\pi r^2 \times 2 - \frac{\sqrt{3}}{4} r^2\right)$

Percentage grazing area = $\dfrac{\frac{1}{6}r^2(4\pi - 3\sqrt{3})}{\pi r^2} \times 100 \approx 39\%$

Chapter 11 GEOMETRY II

— COURSEWORK: Surveying with a Silva compass   page 239

MARKS (M) 1;   (A) 8;   (E) 3;   (N) 3;   (I) 3;   (C) 2

It is most important that all pupils are taught how to measure accurately a magnetic bearing using a 'Silva compass'.

If it does not have a mirror, the compass should be held by one pupil who looks along the side and points it in the right direction. A second pupil then turns the compass housing.

The cheapest Silva compass will not measure angles very accurately and full marks should be given for a tolerance of ±2 degrees. The scale drawings will probably not be very accurate but the skills involved are most worthwhile.

In part 3, X and Y should be marked by the teacher in such a way that pupils can return to the marks in a subsequent lesson. If possible the teacher should take all the necessary bearings using a Silva compass with a mirror, in order to check the pupil's bearings. Otherwise the average of each bearing should be worked out.

Remind the pupils that on each of their drawings they should indicate the scale used and the direction of North and should label each of the corners. The lines on their paper can be used to indicate North.) All bearings should be shown in a suitable table.

The following notes will help in the marking of this Coursework:

Category	*Maximum marks*	*Notes*
Method	1	Percentage error in 2 c.
Accuracy	4	Measurement of bearings.
	4	Scale drawing.
Explanation	3	
Neatness	3	
Initiative	3	Diagrams showing the intersection of two bearings from a short base and at an acute angle. See below.
Content	2	Comment on the factors which affect the accuracy of a Silva compass. These should include: narrow protractor on housing, oscillating needle, short length (side of compass) to line up the direction, possible interference of nearby metal railings or posts.

Bearings intersecting at a point P, from a small base AB and a longer base XY.

Two bearings from A, which differ by 2°, intersecting with a bearing from B.

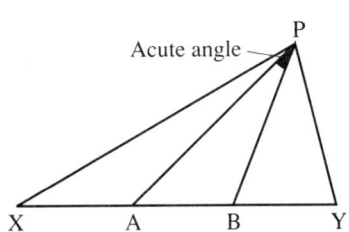
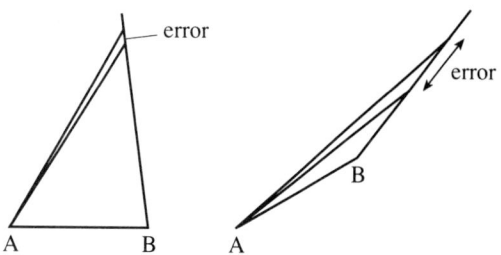

79

Chapter 11 GEOMETRY II

▬ FACT FINDERS: Wimbledon   page 240

1 Current year − 1877

2 **a** 21.1% approximately   **b** 21.1% approximately   **c** 43.1% approximately

3 £3450 + 0.5 × £94230 = £50 565

4 £85 500 + 0.5 × £56 970 = £113 985

5 Time = $\frac{23.78}{(140 \times 1600/3600)}$ = 0.382 seconds

6 Percentage decrease = $\frac{30\,000}{403\,706} \times 100$ = 7.4%

7 $\frac{11.7}{62} \times 100$ = 18.9%

8 Balls/match = $\frac{21\,000}{650}$ ≈ 32 balls

9 Strawberries   £12 × 23 × 10^3 = £276 000
   Tea   £0.50 × 33 × 10^3 = £16 500
   Beer   £1.20 × 75 × 10^3 = £90 000
   Champagne   £25 × 12 × 10^3 = £300 000
   TOTAL   = £682 500

   Amount/person = $\frac{682\,500}{(403\,706 - 30\,000)}$ = £1.83

10 You will probably need to give a reminder that Edberg won but Graf lost, in 1990. Michael wins £50 on Edberg but loses £20 on Graf so his net winnings amount to £30 not including tax!

▬ MULTIPLE CHOICE TEST 3A   page 250

For Chapters 8 to 11.

| 1 a | 2 c | 3 b | 4 d | 5 a | 6 b | 7 b | 8 d | 9 a | 10 c |
| 11 b | 12 c | 13 b | 14 a | 15 b | 16 d | 17 a | 18 c | 19 c | 20 b |

▬ MULTIPLE CHOICE TEST 3B   page 252

For Chapters 8 to 11.

| 1 c | 2 b | 3 b | 4 a | 5 d | 6 d | 7 b | 8 a | 9 b | 10 a |
| 11 a | 12 c | 13 c | 14 d | 15 a | 16 b | 17 a | 18 c | 19 d | 20 c |